THE EBAY BUSINESS HANDBOOK

4TH EDITION

HOW ANYONE CAN STILL BUILD A BUSINESS AND MAKE BIG MONEY ON EBAY.CO.UK

ROBERT PUGH

HARRIMAN HOUSE LTD

18 College Street

Petersfield

Hampshire

GU31 4AD

GREAT BRITAIN

Tel: +44 (0)1730 233870

Email: enquiries@harriman-house.com

Website: www.harriman-house.com

Published in Great Britain in 2015

Copyright © Harriman House Ltd

Paperback ISBN: 9780857194558

eBook ISBN: 9780857194565

British Library Cataloguing in Publication Data

A CIP catalogue record for this book can be obtained from the British Library.

---

eBook edition

As a buyer of *The eBay Business Handbook 4th Edition* you can now download the eBook edition free of charge to read on an eBook reader, smartphone or computer. Simply go to:

http://ebooks.harriman-house.com/ebay4ed

You can then register and download your free eBook.

Follow us on Twitter – **@harrimanhouse** – for the latest on new titles and special offers.

Contents

Sign up to the FREE eBay Bulletin

If this book has helped you with your eBay business and you would like to know even more, why not sign up for my free weekly newsletter and keep up-to-date with the latest developments for eBay sellers. There have been in excess of 300 so far and they are all stored on the website for your perusal. You can also send me your feedback and tell me how this book has kick-started your eBay adventure.

Distributed by Harriman House, the bulletin features essential information such as hints and tips for eBay sellers, sales techniques and advice for moving with the markets, technical developments within eBay, readers' letters ('Ask Molly'), HTML guidance, etc.

For a bit of respite from all the hard work, I will also share some of the more amusing moments from the world of eBay sales. Like the guy who bought an item clearly labelled as half a kilo of Lego and then got in touch to complain about the quantity! And then there are the weird and wonderful auctions that take place online – how much would you bid for an air guitar?

You can also keep up-to-date with my own eBay career; I'll share my experiences, both good and bad.

To sign up to my free newsletter, please visit:
intel.harriman-house.com/eBay-bulletin

About the author

The unofficial bio

It is now nine years since I left the corporate rat race, where I was a salesperson of moderate ability. Aged 40, I had accomplished enough to be able to retire and live a modest lifestyle, perhaps only needing to sell one of my children. The trouble is that a salesperson can never really retire, it is in the blood, so something had to be found to prevent me from being stuck on the sofa, watching *Homes under the Hammer* at 10am each morning (this is actually a great show and would have implications for the Pugh family as time went by).

Having been introduced to eBay a while earlier and having used the site to sell unwanted items for pocket money, I now turned to it anew and this time with the intention to make money. It has been a rocky path at times but now I am a triple PowerSeller (a badge I am still proud to wear) with business interests in cosmetics, toys, DIY materials, clothes and – most recent of all – a venture into electrical fuses. Well, it floats my boat anyway.

My cosmetics business is now registered as a limited company, with an annual turnover target of a quarter of a million pounds. Other interests are more seasonal but contribute significantly to the rehousing fund of my many daughters (or Elves, as they are often described).

It has been nine years of constant selling; I have shifted over 100,000 items. Earnings from these endeavours are not that important to me, as life is after all just a game and money the means of keeping score. You will still see me on a Sunday morning scouring the car boot sales along the A12 corridor looking for that elusive 'Harrison lesser watch'.

As I expand my knowledge I pass it on to anybody who is interested. I still try to write an eBay-related bulletin each week, with current news and wacky stories as told to me by my readers. With over nine years' worth of these bulletins now stored online there must be something of use in there somewhere for all eBay users.

The other main influence in my peculiar lifestyle is the publisher of this tome – Harriman House. During a relationship lasting what feels like a lifetime they have steered me through the maze that is publishing, introduced me to the media and given me a spell checker to die for. These guys also edit my weekly bulletins and distribute to thousands of expectant readers each time.

It is a scary thing speaking on your first radio show, and a two-hour live phone-in at 10pm in Liverpool without any notes is a tad daunting. I must say here and now that all the media attention has not changed me at all, even my brief appearance on *Crimewatch* [Ed: he means *Newsnight*].

Please do enjoy this book. I hope it sparks something – whether it be a new hobby or a profitable business – and remember my motto is *get rich slowly*.

The official bio

Bob is married with three daughters, a useless Shih Tzu dog and an extremely active coffee machine called Kylie!

After 24 years working for the same company, and many years within the corporate sales division, Bob realised it was time for a change. He began selling on eBay in January 2003, initially by clearing his house of unwanted items. When he started out he had very little knowledge of computers and no experience of selling via the internet. The first few months proved to be a steep learning curve, but he soon mastered the systems and became an established eBay triple PowerSeller.

Since this book was first published, Bob has made numerous media appearances to share his expert eBay knowledge and has received plenty of positive feedback. For example:

> "eBay is now a part of life, it's changed people's lives completely and has made so much money, for so many people. Bob was so enthusiastic on-air and actually taught me a hell of a lot about eBay – and what a great book he has written too."

> **Pete Price, Presenter, Radio City**

Bob's second book, *eBay Q&A – 200 of the most popular questions about eBay*, was published in September 2007 by Harriman House.

eBay Selling Success was Bob's third book, published in May 2012, and is available as an eBook from all good digital retailers.

Bob writes a free, weekly newsletter offering tips, advice and real-life stories about the world's most famous online marketplace. Sign up today at: intel.harriman-house.com/eBay-bulletin

Preface

This book will take you from the very first act of choosing your eBay username through to the creation of your own business.

The process is very easy; to sell on eBay is not complicated and requires no sales experience. However, to use eBay to its full potential, to maximise returns and develop a robust online business, does require an understanding of sales, marketing and business processes. You will find thoughts and techniques to help you within these pages.

Who the book is for

This book has been written for anyone who has ever considered the idea of running their own eBay business and being their own boss. Whether you want to supplement an existing income, or you want a complete change of career, this book is for you.

This handbook is intended as an introduction to successful eBay selling. It shows you how to start in a small way and then grow at your own pace to a level you choose. No knowledge of running a business, sales techniques or computers is assumed. These areas are covered to a level that will enable you to be successful, without becoming bogged down with technical detail. You will not require a grasp of complex industry jargon; all that's required is an open mind and a desire to succeed.

This book also contains more advanced ideas for anyone with an existing eBay business. With a fresh, common sense approach to selling, there are many hints, tips and personal recommendations that can be applied to your eBay activities.

What the book covers

This book provides you with everything you need to know to get started on eBay as a seller, or improve your sales and profit if you already trade. It is structured in a logical way, from the most basic planning in the early stages through to more complicated day-to-day tasks like managing paperwork.

Unlike other eBay books, this handbook is based on my personal experience as an established PowerSeller. Everything from the practical concerns of international sales to the purchase of packing materials is covered here.

I will show how I went from zero to a feedback score of 25,000 in the first five years and then to over 53,000 feedbacks and counting. From the very first LP record to the family car, I have sold items to almost every corner of the globe, taken every form of payment known to man, and personally packed a huge variety of items. Anybody can do this: just follow the steps in this book, dedicate the time, set your own goals and persevere until you achieve them.

Structure of the book

The development of an eBay business can be achieved in several stages and the chapters of the book reflect this; they follow a logical progression that allows you to evolve at your own speed, from the very first idea to building your business for the future.

At each stage, references are made to my own experiences of selling on eBay. I highlight the pitfalls I've encountered along the way and some of the more interesting ways to make selling both enjoyable and very rewarding.

Here is what you will find as you read on:

How to get started

Areas covered in the chapter 'Starting Out' include:
- What eBay is all about.
- What equipment you will need to get started and how much this is likely to cost.
- Considering the items you are going to sell. What kinds of things can be sold and what should be avoided? How do you conduct market research?
- What feedback is and detailed seller ratings (DSRs) are.
- How to research your chosen market, discover what is currently selling and how your would-be competitors are doing. Searching eBay is a key element to successful trading – learn how best to use the system to your advantage.
- Where to find stock.
- When to sell and what time commitments are involved.
- Creating your seller account: choosing the right name and thinking about whether to register as a business seller.
- How big your market should be and whether you should sell overseas.
- The eBay fee structure and the Top-rated seller fee discount scheme.

Preparing for the first listing

This chapter looks at the preliminary work you need to do before you make your first listing live. It covers:

- How to check out the competition: find out what is selling and what is not fetching the price it ought to. See how the item you are going to be selling has been doing when other sellers have sold it recently.

- The areas for initial thought as you plan your listings.

- Your trading terms and conditions.

- What payment methods you must and can choose to offer.

- Guidelines on how to prepare your item for listing.

- What packing materials you will need, where best to obtain them and how much they will cost.

- How to post your item, which carrier to use, how much it is likely to cost and how to package the item to ensure a safe delivery.

- Advice and examples on saving pictures of your items on your computer and how to edit them to improve them.

- The 'Best Match' ranking of eBay search results.

Creating your first listing

This chapter is a step-by-step guide to creating an item listing on eBay, with hints and tips at every stage. It looks at:

- What you really need to know to sell your first item.

- How to get the maximum number of people to see your item by placing your listing in the correct category on eBay.

- Choosing the best title. Without a good title, nobody will find your item in the first place.

- The description of your item. This is what will convince the visitor to do business with you. This section looks in detail at various techniques you can use to describe your item.

- What to consider when choosing the start price for your listings. How long should you allow your listing to run, when should you start it and should you use a reserve price?

- Loading your pictures on to eBay.

- Extra options available to promote your item.

While a listing is live

- What is likely to happen while the item is listed for sale, what kind of contact you might get from potential customers and how to deal with this.

- You may decide to revise your listing details, cancel bids or even remove the listing altogether. The processes you will need to follow are described.

After a listing has ended

The end of your listing marks the beginning of the next phase in the sales process. This section covers:

- How to sell more items to second and third-placed bidders; the Second Chance Offer is explained.

- What to consider when packaging your item to ensure a safe delivery.

- The various issues surrounding dispatch, along with recommendations on best practice.

- How to claim back eBay fees should your buyer default.

Refine your listing format

Now the basics of how to create listings have been covered, it is time to take your listsings to the next level, following these steps:

- Create your own appearance and design your own page format.

- With fully worked examples, this section shows how to include larger pictures at no extra cost, provide live links to other websites and promote your other items. All of this is possible with little or no previous knowledge of creating websites or internet content.

- Fully customise your listings using basic HTML (the code language that is used to write websites). Alter the colour of your pages and create your own backgrounds and borders. All the code you need and an explanation of how to use it can be found in this section.

Fraud

Whenever money changes hands there is the opportunity for fraud. This section will highlight the issues around:

- Payment fraud. How to anticipate this situation, what to check for and precautions you should take.

- The possible hijack of your eBay account. You will encounter various attempts by third parties to obtain your eBay password and take control of your account. We look in detail at the systems used to guard against these scams and how to spot potential dangers.

- What eBay will and won't do concerning fraud and how you should proceed if anything goes wrong.

- What to do if you are the victim of fraud. How to put things right with minimum hassle.

Developing your business

Develop your online business and build your eBay brand. This chapter discusses options to maximise your eBay business for increased sales and higher profits. There are comprehensive sections on:

- eBay shops. You will find out what options are available, how much they cost and what advantages you can expect to see. There is also an insight into the various seller tools that are available and how these enhancements can be used to encourage repeat sales from satisfied customers.

- How to increase the exposure of your listings and your cash flow by becoming an eBay Affiliate. What is involved, what the benefits really are and how you can make money by passing business to eBay from your own website.

- PowerSeller status. What it means and how to make the grade. Is it really good for sales?

- Trading with the global economy. This can appear to be a minefield of red tape and regulations. It is possible to export from the UK with minimum stress and this section outlines the requirements.

Managing paperwork

Keeping on top of the paperwork in any business is a demanding task and an eBay business is no different. This last section of the book looks at:

- The legal issues surrounding business on the internet and how these impact on requirements such as VAT.

- What your position is regarding tax; both income and capital gains tax will be explained.

- Becoming self-employed. This section delves into more detail about self-employment, how easy it is to register and what it means for things such as National Insurance.

- Your tax return. With any business comes the need to submit final accounts to HMRC (Her Majesty's Revenue & Customs) once a year. This section highlights some of the typical costs of an eBay business and provides guidance for calculating your profit.

Introduction

Have you ever wondered what it would be like to be your own boss, to work when you decide to and make as much money as you want? Perhaps you would like to work from home, spend more time with the children and, at the same time, create a business that could grow as large as you wish. I wanted this and after just two years selling on eBay I had all of these things.

Following a long career in the world of corporate sales, I became disillusioned and realised that I yearned for a different way of life. Now, nine years on, I have left full-time work and concentrate my time and energy on eBay. I work when I want to; when the sun shines I don't have to work at all. After almost 20 years driving along the motorways of the UK, I can now smile to myself when I hear of traffic jams and congestion as I make another coffee and walk to my office.

My story is not unique by any means; there are thousands of people earning good money from eBay. Some just want to supplement their existing income, some to own their own business and others, such as myself, want a complete change.

I achieved PowerSeller status in just two years from a standing start and I have learnt so much along the way. I have developed a complete end-to-end process that allows me to sell everything from an unwanted CD to the garden shed. Everything I know about selling on eBay is in this book. If you want to change your lifestyle a little, or maybe make a completely fresh start, this book will help you get there.

ONE

A DAY IN THE LIFE OF AN EBAY TRADER

Dear Diary...

It has been quite a while since my last diary entry and an interesting couple of years. I have chosen to describe how I would be occupied on a typical Sunday during August when the weather is set fair.

Alarm clocks are a long distant memory for me during the working week – from Monday to Friday I regard 9am as a civilised time to rise. Sundays during the boot sale season are a more hectic affair, with the alarm set very early.

5am – And so it begins, just another day in the office

Kettle on, iPad on and skates on. It is a mad rush with coffee on the go and, depending upon how many children are present, a queue for the shower. Did I mention that all my offspring are female? The deadline is 6am and today we are on time; it should be a great day.

6am – En route

Time to check the business; not me, I hasten to add, I'm driving. Mrs Mollybol is in charge of all things technical, including the iPad, as I'm still using a Nokia 3310!

Cosmetic sales overnight were par for the course. I no longer ship these lines overseas so overnight sales are no longer the source of excitement they used to be. I'll explain why I only sell cosmetics in the UK later in this book.

Toys and DIY items are, however, available worldwide and this morning they amount to a Meccano motor, two bags of Lego, 40 plastic 'Gogos', a 'Build A Bear' rabbit, two 40-amp fuses and a two port zone valve. An eclectic mix. It gives me a good start to the day at £95 and it's a lot more interesting than mascara and lipstick.

6.30am – Arrive at the first boot sale of the day

If all goes to plan we should hit three boot sales this morning and be in a coffee shop somewhere by 11.30. Boot sales are where it all started for me and they still hold a place in my heart. There's the promise of something special, or a whole car load of goodies, and this is enough to drive me on.

The shopping list today includes all the usual suspects. For my toy business it's Lego, Playmobil, Warhammer, Fisher-Price and anything else that catches my eye. For the DIY business I am looking for the electrician who is clearing out his van and the plumber who just wants shot of his stash of spares; all of these items can find a home in my eBay stores.

This week the team also have another shopping list due to an ongoing project: a kitchen sink, bath panel, assorted light fittings, two radiators, paint, laminate flooring and curtain tracks. All these items should be here at a fraction of the retail cost.

So, a little like Fagin, I send off my Elves to forage.

Before too long it's back to the car with armfuls of junk, I mean valuable merchandise. As they say, one man's rubbish…

With over 25 years' worth of combined experience the Molly clan sure can spot a bargain. The kitchen sink (new bowl and a half, stainless steel) can be ticked off the list, a snip at £25. Two unused 900mm-wide radiators at £15 for the pair and a pack and a half of laminate flooring underlay for £4 are also acquired. There is of course the usual mix of toys and other saleable items as well.

Although the total sales value of items from car boot sales is around 25% of cosmetic sales the buzz of the hunt makes it worthwhile and turnover of £60k+ for a morning's work each week for seven months does have a certain attraction.

8.00am – Off we go again

Our first boot sale was in Colchester and the next stop is just outside Chelmsford. We have a quick loo stop at M&S Simply Food, grab a latte and onwards we go. Replying to customer questions is a chore but it's best dealt with in dead time, so out comes the iPad once more. Two Elves with us in the car today are both on their own tablets checking their respective eBay businesses. If you can imagine a cottage industry in a Ford Focus then you get the idea.

8.30ish – Arrive at Boreham, a huge car boot sale beside the A12

This second boot sale is much the same as the last one but this time we are later and the whole mood changes. No longer are we competing with other dealers for the best-selling items – now it is more of a leisurely stroll in the park. (Leisurely that is within the time constraints of the next boot sale entry, which as a 'late riser' is 10am. It's a 20-minute drive to get there, via McDonald's for a coffee top up.)

The haul here is ok. The chances of finding that lost master are long gone as certain telly programmes and the instant market valuation provided by eBay mean that almost everybody knows the value of their items.

The trick is to identify those people that either don't know or can't be bothered to sell online. Items of note include a crate of old electrical fuses for £35, which on the face of it is not that exciting, but if you needed a new fuse for your shower or solar panels then a £10 fuse from yours truly could save you £500 for a new fuse board. I sell around a dozen fuses every day and they are posted as large letters, which is even better (you'll find out why later in the book).

The bath panel also turns up at the car, new in box from the Bathstore for £10. Another one ticked off the shopping list!

9.30am – Towards Southend for a 10am kick off

10am – Arrive at the last of the day's car boots

As the buyers are held in check until 10am it does resemble the start of the Grand National when the tape goes up. People actually run, such are the huge rewards that can be obtained. I am not into running and I must stress that I don't lean into car windows asking for jewellery or mobile phones. I am a *gentleman trader*, it is just the way I was brought up.

11.30ish – It's all over, off to Costa

It has now become a tradition to roughly value the day's purchases over a large Mocha and a Rocky Road snack bar. Of course there are fees involved and a lot of time sorting, listing and packing, but the headline retail value for the contents of the car is around the £1,200 mark.

1.30pm – Home again, home again

The fun part is sorting out the wheat from the chaff and when we get home and unload the loot the front room takes on a look akin to Del Boy's lock up. Although there are currently 75 cosmetic items and a host of toys awaiting postage these are ignored; let's face it, playing with a whole load of new toys is much more fun.

As usual there is an abundance of Thomas the Tank Engine trains and track, most of which is sold from a *multi-variation listing* (more about this later) so the online inventory can be quickly updated with today's purchases. For any items sold within the last 90 days the old listing record can be retrieved and added back on to eBay as a new item, so we spend time doing this, too. Also at this juncture I scribble down a list of what was bought for resale and how much it cost. This is a chore but it pays dividends at the end of the fiscal year – I'll explain why later.

4pm – Tea time

All good things have to come to an end and tea time is as good a time as any to take a short break. Mollybol HQ runs along traditional lines with pit stops at 11am for coffee and 4pm for afternoon tea. At these times any kids present are forced to speak to their parents, which can be a rarity these days.

4.30pm – Time to knuckle down

It is now time to get on with the packing of items sold in the last few hours. The more envelopes written today the easier will be the Monday rush.

I have been raising funds for another project and running a four-day sale on toys and DIY – this is dead easy to do with an eBay shop, I'll expand on it later. Suffice to say that there are a lot of items that need packing and this is by far the worst part of an eBay business.

Across all the shops and product ranges I shift around 18,000 items per year. All this processing is still achieved in-house with help from the Elves and any of their boyfriends who come calling; here's a cup of tea, a biscuit, a roll of sticky tape, brown paper and a kilo of Lego – enjoy.

Lipsticks and mascaras are easy, most lines fit inside a bubble bag so although tedious the throughput is very high. Toys are altogether different and take a lot longer to process. The only problem I have with lipsticks is that they are often similar colours (what exactly is the difference between 'sunbronze' and 'mulberry'?) and the writing is very small so mistakes do happen!

No relaxing Sunday afternoon for the Molly household; this is the working week condensed into one day. Apart from two hours or so each day to keep on top of postage and listing items as and when the mood takes me I can take the rest of the time off – you know it makes sense.

TWO

STARTING OUT

Overview

They do say that even the longest journey must begin with an initial step, which in the case of an eBay business is certainly true. The great thing about starting an online business and selling on eBay is that you control how long the journey will be and how fast you want to travel.

Private sellers on eBay no longer need any money to get started, as auction listings starting at 99p are free to add to the site. All you need is an unwanted gift or two and you are in business.

WHAT IS A LISTING?

A listing is how we describe an item for sale on eBay. Listings come in two main varieties:

1. **Auction**: Items are open for bids from eBay users. The highest bidder at the end of the auction wins the item, just as in a traditional auction.

2. **Buy It Now (BIN)**: These listings have a fixed price. Users have the option to purchase them immediately, just as you would in a normal shop.

Some eBay options relate only to the auction format and some are specific to BIN. However, most of the advice in this book will apply to both unless stated otherwise.

How big your business grows will depend on many things. The beginning, however, will be a similar experience for the largest corporate undertaking or the smallest sole trader with only the germ of an idea of what they want to do.

When I started out on eBay, I charged straight into selling. I had not bought anything on eBay before and did not understand anything about the site. I have learned and adapted over time, but I can't help thinking how many mistakes I could have avoided with a little more preparation in the early days. With that in mind, this section is about some of the things you will need to know before you start to sell on eBay.

This chapter introduces you to eBay, how it was formed and how big it really is, who sells on eBay, what sells on eBay and just why eBay is the ideal medium to fulfil your ambitions. Included are thoughts about:

- What you could sell.
- Who you could sell to.
- What you will have to pay in eBay fees when your items sell.

There are many websites offering help to newbie eBay sellers. They may not be for you and any advice that has to be purchased should be carefully considered.

The site **www.easyauctionbusiness.com** is an example, take a look and judge for yourself.

What exactly is eBay?

eBay used to be called 'Auction Web', later they tried to register the name 'EchoBay.com' but it was taken by a mining company – so it was shortened to 'eBay'.

eBay is an online marketplace that enables trade nationally and internationally. It was founded in the USA in 1995 and was originally intended as a website where collectors of various items such as Pez sweet dispensers and Beanie Babies could trade. It has grown to become much more: millions of items are traded every day and almost anything that is legal can be bought and sold on the site.

To say that eBay is big hardly does it justice; eBay is huge and it is still growing. There are now hundreds of millions of registered users. It is truly global and allows any member in any country where eBay operates to trade with any other member. On any given day there are millions of items for sale, in areas including antiques, toys, books, computers, sporting goods, photography and cars.

My best purchase to date has been an assembled kitchen complete with sink, taps, worktop and even a small fridge for £65. I had no need for the fridge so that was put back on eBay and sold for £50. The kitchen has now been reinstalled and looks great. Not bad for £15!

eBay in figures

Some facts and figures that help give an idea of the world of eBay:

- High-value items sold through eBay include a private business jet for $4.9 million in 2001, a baseball card for $1.1 million in 2000 and an 83-acre town in California including eight houses, a cafe and a post office, which sold for $1.77 million in 2002.

- eBay.co.uk has 14 million registered active users and is growing each year.

- There were over 112 million active users worldwide as of Q4/2012.

- eBay enabled more than $175 billion of commerce globally in 2012.

eBay.co.uk

Founded in October 1999, eBay.co.uk is now one of the largest online marketplaces in the UK. Over 40% of active internet users visit eBay.co.uk once a month.

On eBay UK:

- There are up to 10 million items for sale at any one time.

- The number of registered users is fast approaching 20 million.

- There are over 13,000 item categories.

- Around 180,000 professional sellers in the UK use eBay as a primary or secondary source of income.

- There are over 13,000 *Featured shops* in the UK (this will be explained later in the book).

An average day

On an average day on eBay UK, someone buys a:

- Mobile phone every 21 seconds.

- Laptop every two minutes.

- MP3 player every two minutes.

- Car every two minutes.

- Woman's handbag every 36 seconds.

The eBay community

The eBay community is made up of buyers and sellers who visit the site to trade. This might include large companies, small companies, individuals running businesses from home, or those just trying to clear out an attic.

The members of this collective each have a common goal: to buy and sell in a pleasant and rewarding environment. The community is self-policing and users frequently form 'neighbourhood watch' groups to help guard against misuse or violations of site etiquette.

 Anyone who is over 18 can register on eBay and within a short while they can buy or sell.

Information and knowledge is freely exchanged between members via a number of user forums or discussion boards. The discussion forums are found under the 'Community' tab. Almost any question can be posted and anybody browsing through the forums can choose to reply – both question and answer are available for all to see and learn from.

There are discussion boards for a whole range of issues: one specifically for new users, one about postage and payments, and even a discussion board for HTML concerns. Through the discussion boards, members meet and get to know each other, discuss topics of mutual interest and help each other to learn all about eBay. PowerSellers have a dedicated discussion board where more complex issues can be discussed. Many PowerSellers also patrol the general forums offering their experience to those who ask.

When starting out on your selling career with eBay, refer back to these boards from time to time. If you have a problem it is certain that someone else will have faced a similar concern before and you may just find the answer here.

eBay encourages open and honest communication between the community and the company. Although this sometimes falls down in practice the intention is sound at least. Members of the community often give their feedback to improve the environment in which they spend their time.

The fundamental principle of eBay is that every trader, whether large or small, has the same set of rules for trading. With the exception of volume-related discounts and benefits for top sellers, it is a fairly level playing field.

eBay can easily become part of a member's lifestyle. Many members have created second businesses, or left day jobs altogether, by trading on eBay. For hundreds of thousands of others, eBay is the place to share a passion for items that are collectable or special in some way.

In the Pugh household it is truly a family affair with all three Elves using eBay to save money and raise funds. They grew up in a sales environment and were exposed to the concepts of profit and loss from an early age, so it's natural for them to use the site. eBay sort of binds the family together, even if just in the form of the occasional plea for bubble bags or stamps.

 Any of eBay's millions of worldwide members could have access to your listings and could become your customers. These eBay members could also be your competitors as they can market to the UK in the same way that you can direct your sales to another country.

The eBay values

eBay was founded on five key values and eBay.co.uk holds these at its heart. As with all systems, there will be those who break the rules and go against the interests of the community. However these amount to only a very small proportion of eBay users. With a little caution and some help from the recommendations in this book, you will be able to avoid most pitfalls and trade successfully in an environment where problems are very much the exception.

The five key eBay values are:

1. eBay believe that people are basically good.

2. eBay recognises and respects everyone as a unique individual.

3. eBay believes everyone has something to contribute.

4. eBay encourages people to treat others the way that they want to be treated.

5. eBay believes that an honest, open environment can bring out the best in people.

Reading these values for the first time can seem a little strange (and might seem rather too American for British tastes!), but after you have been involved with the site for some time you will find that the community at large generally upholds these values.

The equipment you need

Placing an item for auction on eBay could cost you absolutely nothing, but this does not take into account the costs of the other equipment that is required. It is important to understand what equipment you will need, who supplies it and, most importantly, how much it is likely to cost. The size of your business will determine the cost of starting out, but even someone using eBay at a very basic level will need the following:

1. Computer.

2. Digital camera.

3. Internet connection.

4. Security software.

1. Computer

You need an up-to-date computer or device that will connect to the internet. These start from about £400 (or cheaper on eBay!) for a desktop PC and a little more for a laptop. Old computers will work, but may have some restrictions in terms of not being able to use the latest software, etc.

It may be worth considering the purchase of a second-hand computer if funds are tight. Also, the widespread use of smartphones has now made it possible to run a business from just about anywhere.

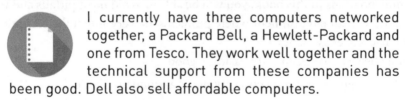 I currently have three computers networked together, a Packard Bell, a Hewlett-Packard and one from Tesco. They work well together and the technical support from these companies has been good. Dell also sell affordable computers.

Recent additions to the technology stable include an MSI Netbook, an HTC android phone and an iPad mini. All these clever toys have one purpose – to keep me permanently connected to eBay and help me make money.

The hub of my home network is a Sky wireless router. All my PCs work with it as well as the kids' laptops when they return home.

Internet browser software

If you are having trouble with Microsoft Internet Explorer or the Outlook Express email software then try the Mozilla Firefox internet browser and Mozilla Thunderbird email client. I have now loaded these on to all computers at Molly HQ (the affectionate name for my garden shed, a haven from the stresses of day-to-day life!). I have found them fast, easy to use and – my favourite – they are both free.

Reference

- Mozilla (www.mozilla.org).
- Hewlett-Packard (www.hp.co.uk).
- Packard Bell (www.packardbell.co.uk).
- Dell (www.dell.co.uk).

2. Digital camera

Back in the early days I didn't even have a camera, many listings didn't have any pictures at all and yet things still sold. It is a lot easier today.

A good-quality picture will enhance your eBay listings. A mid-range digital camera will start from around £70 and go up to around £150. Prices go much higher than this for advanced models!

I tend to buy last year's model, rather than a brand new one, when my camera needs replacing (which it does after every 6,000 pictures or so).

For more detail, see the sections on cameras and photographs later in the book.

3. Internet connection

A broadband internet connection is now a must, and at around £10 per month it's a small price to pay. Check to see if you can get a faster connection as the extra speed is well worth the investment. Broadband is offered by a number of suppliers and can be delivered via ADSL, cable or satellite links. To find out if your home or office can accept broadband use: www.broadbandchecker.co.uk

Check with your broadband supplier about any download limits. Some providers may have a monthly limit with their basic package and, if exceeded, the service could cost you more than you think.

A high data speed on your mobile device can also make the eBay experience more rewarding, unless you are using it while travelling along the A12, as nothing seems to work very well there.

The major broadband suppliers are:

- BT Broadband (www.bt.com/broadband)
- EE (www.ee.co.uk/broadband).
- Plusnet (www.plus.net).
- Sky(www.sky.com/broadband).
- TalkTalk (www.TalkTalk.co.uk/broadband)
- Virgin Media (www.virginmedia.com/broadband)

 If you take your broadband service and phone line from Sky in addition to your TV subscription the broadband costs just £10 per month.

Sky recently offered me a free upgrade to a faster router; it was easy to install and has a better range. The old one – as you may have guessed – was sold on eBay for £20. Nice one Sky.

4. Security software

The threat posed by the internet to unprotected computers is very real. Antivirus, firewall and other security software are required to stop rogue programs attacking your computer. Some of this software can be downloaded directly from the internet with no charge. Below I will deal with the different types of threat and give some suggestions as to protection that can be used.

Tips for safe computing

With all the bad press concerning viruses and computers crashing, it can seem inevitable that your computer will be affected in some way. You can minimise these risks by taking certain precautions. Practice *safe surfing* and you should remain free from infection!

- Be suspicious of attachments that arrive on emails from unknown sources.

- Some viruses can send emails and attachments that appear to have been sent by people you know. If in any doubt, confirm with the sender that they did in fact send you the email.

- Do not set your email program to auto-run attachments.

- Keep your computer fully updated with the latest security software.

- Back up all of your important data regularly and keep the back up copies in a safe location (somewhere different to the computer, ideally).

Security software

I recommend:

- Malwarebytes (www.malwarebytes.org): Works alongside anti-virus software to identify unwanted programs. Free version available.

- Hitmanpro (www.surfright.nl/en/hitmanpro): A second-opinion virus scanner which could find something others have missed. Free 30-day trial available.

- AdwCleaner (toolslib.net/downloads/viewdownload/1-adwcleaner): Free removal tool for getting rid of/preventing:

  - Adware (ad software).

  - PUP/LPI (potentially undesirable program).

  - Toolbars.

  - Hijacker (hijack of the browser's homepage).

 I use a software program called CA Anti-spyware. It costs about £20 and works with my anti-virus software and firewall. You can check this out at: www.pestpatrol.com

What can be done to cure an infection

No matter how safe you make your computer and how vigilant you are, there is the chance that your system will become infected. If you suspect that something is wrong, run all of the anti-virus programs that you have installed. This may remove the problem. Some infections are easy to remove, others require more serious action. There are a range of commercially available programs on the internet which tackle specific types of problem. Failing that you will have to seek help from a local computer technician.

Take your computer for a complete service once a year. This will remove any infections and speed up its operation. You MOT the car, so do the same with your computer. A full service will cost about £100.

What to sell

Almost anything can be sold on eBay – even the kitchen sink (which I sold for my brother-in-law for £150). The main restrictions are that there are some prohibited items and some items are not worth anything. Apart from that, almost everything that has a value can be put up for sale – and it seems that even things that don't appear to have any value can also find buyers. With prices for items starting at just one penny and with a £10 million upper limit, everything will find its own level. In this section I will share my experiences and provide recommendations to get your business off to a flying start.

Consider consumer goods such as CDs, DVDs, clothes or household electronics. These should carry relatively high margins, depending upon your wholesaler.

Deciding what to sell on eBay may be immediately obvious to you. For example, you may already have a hobby that could produce an income. You may already have access to a stock of items and need a way to sell them. But if you do not yet know what to sell, this section should provide a few ideas, here are a few to get you thinking:

- Free items offered in high street stores with a particular purchase. Sell the item at a loss and then make your margin on the freebie.

- Buy the contents of a tradesman's van or shed through a small ad and then sell on the contents – great for plumbing or electrical items.

- Pick up unsold Halloween outfits from your local store on 1 November, keep them for a year and sell them the following October.

 Over the past five years I have sold over 100,000 items, including two garden sheds, a washing machine, a full size Queen Mother armorial flag, a Spike Milligan concert poster, the family car, as well as almost everything in the house that was not nailed down.

I am always trying different things and will, as the saying goes, try anything once, although I have not yet tried to sell autumn leaves, a snowman, genuine mud from a very wet rock festival, a jar of pickle or an empty box, but all of these items have been put up for auction by others – and sold!

The first thing to be aware of is what you are actually allowed to sell on eBay and what items are prohibited. You also need to consider what items are technically allowed but best avoided.

 Sometimes things are not what they seem. Whilst looking for a new line of electrical fuses to sell I came across some very old (I mean vintage) ceramic fuses. They sell for a good price and would cost very little so the margins are fine. However, a little more checking via Google revealed that they contain asbestos, which is not really the area I want to be in, so I moved on.

It is then worth checking what is listed on eBay at the moment to understand what sells in the area you are interested in; you need to do market research. This will provide you with an insight into the viability of your particular product and also make you aware of the techniques used by other eBay sellers.

The other consideration if you are unsure of what to sell is the fees that eBay will charge you each time a sale is made. Check out the section later in this book that looks at final value fees, as the percentage charged by eBay varies depending on the category of the item.

Choose a product you already know something about and enjoy working with. Consider issues such as: how you will acquire your stock, where you will store it and what will be involved with shipping.

Prohibited items

eBay have set out guidelines to help sellers decide if their items may be sold. A very clear list of prohibited items can be found on the eBay help pages (pages.ebay.co.uk/help/policies/items-ov.html). Everything not listed would probably be OK to sell.

As you will see, eBay has three categories for these kinds of items:

1. **Prohibited**: items must not be listed on eBay.

2. **Restricted**: items may be listed under certain conditions.

3. **Potentially Infringing**: items may be in violation of certain copyrights, trademarks or other rights.

Selling alcohol or tobacco on eBay is not allowed under any circumstances. The container may be sold as a collectable item but it has to be shown not to contain any banned substances. Extra pictures showing that the container is empty should prevent eBay from removing your listing.

What will eBay do with prohibited listings?

To quote eBay on this:

"eBay reserves the right to delete any listing that may violate any legal provision or the general principles and values of the community at large, even if the legal provision or principles and values are not explicitly stated on the eBay site."

This basically means that in some cases, eBay will make a judgement as they best see it. Remember that eBay has a strong sense of community and other members will report items that contravene the rules.

Items for special consideration

We have looked at items that are not allowed on eBay, but there are also some other products that have their own issues which are worth bearing in mind before deciding to sell them:

- **Fragile items**. Glass, china and collectables can be fragile and the condition is everything to the avid collector. Consider the implications of more secure packaging on cost and time.

- **Heavy items**. Posting heavy items will cost more money. Sending heavy items overseas, particularly those with a low sales value, may incur higher money transaction fees. These will eat into your profit as eBay fees are calculated on the total amount of money transferred, including the postage charges.

- **Country specific items**. Selling items that are targeted at only one country will restrict your market. Some items, such as DVDs, only work in specific regions.

- **Large items**. Large items may only be suitable for collection, or may require specialist transportation which will cost more to arrange. Consider the implications of any additional packing requirements – will you need non-standard boxes? Can you deliver large items and, if so, within what geographic area? Collection from your home or place of work may be inconvenient and this may restrict your market.

- **High-value items**. The higher the value of your items, the more interest there will be from fraudsters who exploit the system. You are unlikely to be defrauded for a second-hand CD, but a valuable watch or mobile phone might be a target. (There are precautions that can be taken to guard against fraud on eBay and these are covered in a later section.)

When selling an old washing machine with a value of £50 or so, I received a bid from Bradford, some 200 miles away. I had stipulated that the item was for collection only and emailed the bidder to confirm. They seemed happy to make the journey and, although they were later outbid, it did show how far some people will travel to collect.

Beginning to sell

Start by selling something that is easy to describe and post – it does not have to be of high value. This will give you experience of the eBay systems and highlight some improvements that you could make in the future. Once you have mastered the process of selling on eBay, almost anything can be sold in much the same way.

An easy way to start selling and to begin building up a good feedback score is to sell unwanted household items. Don't throw away your old camera – somebody will buy it for spares. Hang on to your empty ink jet cartridges, as they can fetch up to £5 a pair. Even the small complimentary bars of soap that you pick up in hotel rooms have a value on eBay.

The great thing about selling your own surplus items is that any money made from them is a bonus; you are mostly looking to learn about the sales process. You will begin to understand how eBay ticks and also get an idea of how much time it all takes. If you do make some money then you could use this to buy stock as your business grows.

The more sales you make, the higher your feedback score will become, which will begin to build your eBay reputation. Establishing yourself as a trustworthy trader is a key element of a successful eBay business. Your potential buyers have little else to go on except your trading history, recorded within your feedback score. Not only is the numerical value important, but also the comments made by those you have traded with.

If you are just starting out with little feedback, buyers may avoid high-value items you are selling as you have no track record. Once you are established, with good feedback, they will be prepared to pay more for your items.

Feedback and detailed seller ratings

Buyers will mark sellers in **four areas** as part of their feedback report when a transaction has been completed. These are known as the detailed seller ratings

(DSRs) and are represented as orange stars. Keep these ratings high and your items will appear higher in some search results and you may also be entitled to a discount on fees when your turnover grows.

The four areas are:

1. Item as described.

2. Communication.

3. Dispatch time.

4. Postage and packing charges.

The net results are shown as marks out of five. If you provide accurate listings and good customer service you should do well. For postage and packing, if you offer free postage then your DSR score for that area will be five stars.

Sellers can only give positive feedback to buyers, so buyers can grade accordingly and leave candid comments without the fear of reprisals. My DSR grades for the cosmetics shop are currently:

• Item as described – 5.0.

• Communication – 5.0.

• Dispatch time – 4.9.

• Postage and packing charges – 5.0.

Keeping DSR scores above 4.6 is key for any fee discounts – more on this later.

Unbundling collections

If you are going to sell a collection of items, consider selling them in several smaller lots. This may attract more buyers who may not want to buy a whole collection. If you have enough of the item to sell a second batch, make the two lots exactly the same as this will allow you to increase the quantity available or give the option for a *Second Chance Offer*, which will be explained a little later. It will also save you the trouble of taking more pictures for the next auction.

Selling your items one at a time, rather than in a larger lot, may have more appeal to certain collectors. When selling a series of books for example, a collector may be interested in one, but be put off if the listing includes several that they do not need.

I use this approach with train sets, listing the track, stations, trains and scenery separately. The buyer can pick and mix the elements they want.

We live in austere times where money is in short supply; some buyers just don't have the means to buy large quantities. I have adapted my selling to accommodate this and now sell most cosmetic lines in singles whereas in the past I used to sell in larger volumes to cut down on postage costs. Economic circumstances change and you must evolve.

Market research

When giving thought to the items you would like to sell, you need to see who else is in the marketplace.

This section will demonstrate how to find items and users on eBay and give a few ideas of things to look for when viewing other listings.

eBay has its own search engines that appear all over the site. These can be used to find items listed on the site and other users. As with all internet search engines, you type in your search requirements and the results are displayed. On eBay there are basic and advanced search facilities available. I will explain both procedures below.

How eBay users find items

. Items can be found on eBay by using two different methods: you can search for them, either by name or by an item number, or you can browse through the site and see what turns up.

 Approximately 75% of items are found with the search facility; only 25% are found by browsing.

Browsing

When an item is placed on eBay, each seller must select a category, or categories, from a list in which to place their item. There are thousands of different categories available to choose from. (I will go into detail about selecting the best category for your items when I talk about placing your first listing a little later.)

The categories are continually changing: as items become popular, a category is added and as interest fades, categories are removed. The current main categories can be found here: www.ebay.co.uk/sch/allcategories/all-categories

Browsing the site starts from the eBay home page, from where you can follow a link to 'Shop by category'. When you click on a main category, a number of subcategories will be shown. Follow the links to drill down the list of items.

You can browse through the entire subcategory list or select an area of specific interest. Narrowing your selection of category will result in fewer items to browse through. If you were interested in some floor-standing speakers for your Hi-Fi system, for instance, your category selection would be:

Electronics > Sound & Vision > TV & Home Audio Accessories > Speaker Stands & Brackets > Stand

The list of items displayed after you have followed this through will be all the items placed into this category by sellers. It may well include items that don't belong if the seller has chosen the incorrect category. (See Fig 1.)

Fig 1. The results of a browse for floor-standing speakers

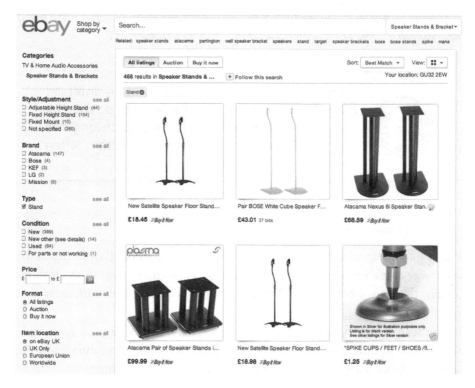

Results display

The results of your browsing can be displayed in a number of ways. The default is to show them by something eBay have termed *Best Match*. Best Match evaluates items and sellers based on a number of factors deemed to be important to buyers, including how well the item matches what the buyer is looking for, its price and postage cost, along with the seller's track record. I will elaborate on some ways sellers can boost their position under the Best Match criteria in 'Chapter 3. Preparing For The First Listing'.

You can alter this display by selecting an alternative from the 'Sort' menu. Among other things, you can sort by *time* (ending soonest or newly listed), *price* (lowest or highest, with or without postage) and *condition* (new or used).

As you will have begun to see by using the browse facility, selecting the incorrect category for an item can have a significant impact on the price that an item reaches. (When I look at placing your first listing in detail in a later chapter, I will discuss this area further.)

Having looked at the browse function, now it is time to understand more about how the other 75% of eBay users find things: they search for them.

eBay shops have their own unique internet address. Items within these shops will be included in searches made by search engines such as Google. I will explain this further when we look at eBay shops in more detail.

Using the search facility

Finding the item you want quickly is a fundamental part of eBay. In much the same way that some shoppers will visit a large town and browse through shops all day, there are others who will want to get the shopping over with as soon as possible.

The search facility within eBay is very efficient. It can be used for simple searches or for quite complex and detailed searches. This section shows how the search facilities work, including some of the more unusual options.

You must anticipate how bidders are going to find your item. Imagine yourself in their position – how would you search for the items you are selling?

Simple search

Simple search engines are on almost every page on eBay. An example of what they look like is shown in Fig 2.

Fig 2. Simple search engine

To do a search, type in the name of the item you are looking for and click the search button. Typing in a general word such as 'bucket' will return thousands of results – 71,845 when I tried it. Finding the particular type of bucket you want from this size of list would be very difficult.

Changing the search to 'plastic bucket' returns a smaller list: in this case only 4,472 items to look through. Change the countries that you want to look at (there's a click box option down the left side of the page) to 'UK only' then the number reduces again to 3,529. The more specific the search, the fewer results are displayed and the easier it is to find an item.

Another example.

This time I'm searching for 'golf clubs'. I see there are 51,793 active listings with the words 'golf clubs' in the title. I can narrow this search further as the results are shown by the category that they are placed in. I am actually looking for a vintage golf club and there are only 1,395 such listings, mainly within the 'Golf Memorabilia' category.

As you can see, this search function is very basic. It will just return listings which contain the search words in the title.

 eBay searches are not case-sensitive, so whether you use capital letters or not, your results will be the same.

Advanced search

Links to the advanced search engine appear next to the simple search box – just click on the link and a whole new set of search options will be available. If there is not a link to the advanced search on the page you are viewing just click the main 'Search' button once and it will appear.

These advanced search options can be combined to allow for a more focused search, or they can be used one at a time. I have shown what I consider to be the most useful advanced search options in Figure 3.

Fig 3. Advanced search engine

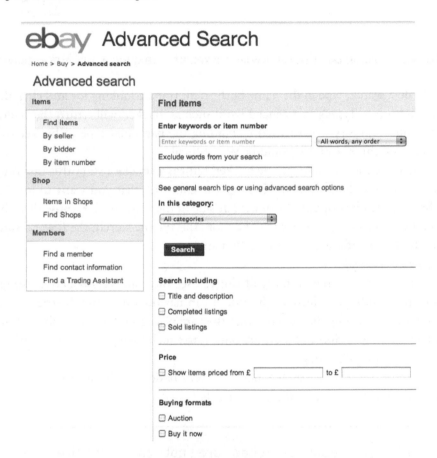

If you choose to include **'Title and description'** in your search then, as the name suggests, eBay will search for your keywords both in the title and in the description of the item. With this option selected, the previous search for 'plastic bucket' now returns 3,498 results. This search enhancement is only available for active listings.

When selling items, ensure that your description contains all the keywords that describe your item. Even if you cannot fit them into the title, put them in the description.

If you narrow the search by selecting **Buy It Now** your results will show the listings with your search words in the title that have the option for an instant purchase.

The results shown from the bucket search were quite diverse, as any listing with the words 'plastic' and 'bucket' somewhere in the description would have been shown. This can be overcome by telling eBay to search for your keywords in a specific way. These techniques can save a lot of time when searching:

- To search for **two or more words somewhere in the title in no particular order** enter the words separated with a space. This is how the previous examples I have shown worked.

- If the **words you are looking for need to be in a particular order**, e.g. War of the Worlds, type the words within quotation marks: "War of the Worlds". Only items with this exact phrase will be shown.

- If you are searching for **items that don't contain one particular word** – for example, hiking boots, but not brown ones – type in the search words 'hiking boots' and then the word 'brown' with a minus sign immediately in front of it, i.e. 'hiking boots -brown'. This will show all listings with 'hiking boots' in the title, except those that also have the word 'brown' in the title.

- If you are searching for **items that do not contain several words** – maybe pottery items, but not Denby, Poole or Wedgwood – place the words you do not want inside brackets and separate them with commas. The search would look like this: "pottery -(Denby, Poole, Wedgwood)".

- To search for **listings that began or will end within a certain time frame**, use the boxes that allow you to stipulate the time frame of listings. For example, you could search for listings that started within the last three hours, or that will end in the next three days.

- Perhaps the most interesting of the advanced search options are the 'Completed listings' and 'Sold listings'. As before, enter your search words into the box and now tick 'Completed listings'. The results shown will be for all of the items which ended in the past 15 days containing your search words. This list will also contain items that did not sell – by selecting the 'Sold listings' option only listings which ended with a sale will be shown. As a seller it is very important to know how popular an item is likely to be before you buy 500 of them from your wholesaler. This search should help you when you are out and about, and this is where a smartphone starts to pay for itself. When I see an item at a car boot sale, or elsewhere, I can access eBay immediately, check out its popularity and decide if a purchase is worthwhile. Bear in mind that a Buy It Now listing may not actually end when a sale is made. If items remain unsold in the listing (as one listing can have a number of items within it) it will not appear in 'Sold listings'. To find these you need to be searching for active or completed listings (leave 'Sold listings' unticked). As auctions have a tendency to fall short of the price asked in fixed price listings you should select the 'Buy It Now' option to get a better idea of the true potential of the item.

Top tips for successful searches

- Use different combinations of search words. Imagine which words a seller might use to describe their item. Try several different phrases and combinations.

- For an even more precise search, state the brand/colour/model of the item. To find a 1980s model of R2-D2 from Star Wars, your search could be: "Star Wars R2D2 1980 Lucas Films".

- Search titles and descriptions to get more matches. You will get more results by searching in title and description. There are only 55 characters of space in the title box, so sellers often cannot fit all of the keywords in and will add them into the description.

- Punctuate correctly. Punctuation marks, such as the hyphen in 't-shirt' should only be included in the search if you expect it to be in the item description. A lot of sellers will not include it.

Further market research

There is a comprehensive web tool available to help with your market research – the eSources Market Research Wizard (research.esources.co.uk/intro/2.php).

This will provide everything you need to know about a particular product or line, including at what times of the year it sells best. If you know the best time to sell, you can better judge when to buy and hold stock for a shorter time – which is great for cash flow.

One of the most interesting aspects of the tool is the ability to assess how your competition is doing with the same product. You can find out:

- The success rate existing eBay sellers have had when selling particular products.

- The selling options that will attract the highest selling price.

- Exactly when to start your auction, when to end it, at what price to begin, in which category to list it and which keywords to use within your listings.

- Which eBay advanced features result in more sales and hence which ones are worth spending money on.

What to look for when searching

As you search through eBay, imagine yourself in the position of a buyer. How do you feel when you see other sellers' listings? Would you place a bid or buy the item? The key to successful selling is to try and understand things from the buyer's point of view. It is not enough to believe that you have the best looking listing and that everything is just great, if, for some reason, buyers do not agree.

Most sellers on eBay will not have given this subject much consideration; they will just list their item without too much thought as to how it looks to their customers. With some planning about the whole environment that you create, you will soon be far ahead of the competition.

 When looking at a listing, make notes of things you like and the things that don't work as well as they should. For each item that you look at, decide if you would in fact trade with the seller. Record your first impressions as these are seldom wrong.

I will now run through some of the areas to pay attention to and which should help with the design of your own eBay listings.

Content

Check the content of the listings you visit. How is the seller promoting their item? Does the description include the seller's terms and conditions? Is the description of the item comprehensive or does it consist of only a few sparse details? Do you feel that the seller cares about the item or is it just another business transaction?

 Check the feedback score of the sellers you find. Is there a difference in the way that experienced sellers present their items as opposed to sellers with less feedback to their name?

Load time

A key factor in constructing a successful auction or fixed-price listing is striking a balance between the amount of content that is included against the amount of time it takes to load the page. The advent of broadband in the UK has made the load time of a page somewhat irrelevant, but until it reaches every home it remains a slight concern. Not every country has broadband internet, so load time could still be an issue for international sellers.

Terms and conditions

Many sellers include their terms and conditions within each listing – you will see many different formats as you search. Look at the tone in which these are presented. Does the seller have hard and fast rules about payment within a certain period of time and do they threaten consequences if you do not meet these terms? How does this make you feel about trading with these sellers?

Other sellers insist that you have a certain number of feedbacks before you bid or will ask that you contact them before placing a bid. Again, how do you feel about this?

Personally, I will not trade with a seller who has created a hostile environment; it is just not a nice place to do business.

Give some thought to the type of conditions you will apply to your listings and how you will present them to potential buyers.

How to find other eBay users

There will be times when you want to find out more information about another eBay user. You may have been asked about a postal charge, but the user forgot to tell you where they are in the world. You may also want to find out more about a user's trading record when considering the removal of a bid they have made on one of your items.

The advanced search facility will allow you to trace other users and find out a little more about them. The process is much the same as a search for items. Start by accessing the advanced search screen. There is a sub-menu on the left side of the page with half a dozen search options available. There are really only three you are likely to need:

1. Find a member.
2. Find items > By seller.
3. Find items > By bidder.

Let's have a look at these in more detail.

1. Find a member

To find an eBay user, just click on the link and type the user's eBay ID into the search box, enter the security check and click search. Just in case you type it incorrectly, eBay will provide any near matches for your search. When the results are shown, just click on the username and their profile details will appear. Fig 4 shows an example of a member profile page. You may need to click on the username a couple of times to get to this page, as the first page that comes up when you click on a member's name is their feedback profile.

Fig 4. Member profile

A user's profile will show their trading history, feedback score and how long they have been a member. As a seller, you are more likely to be interested in their location and how many feedbacks they have. It will also show the history of any name changes that have occurred over time.

As a general rule, the higher number of feedbacks a person has, the more likely they are to complete a trade with no problems as these users know how the system works. Inexperienced bidders can require a little more assistance during the trade, which is why you will sometimes see sellers who do not take bids from new eBay users.

Some countries, such as Germany, have strict rules about the disclosure of personal information. Profile information is not made available until you and your buyers actually enter into a trade.

2. Find items > By seller

This search will find all of the items listed by a specific seller and is great for checking on the competition.

It works in much the same way as the 'Find a member' search but there is the additional ability to include listings that have been completed during the last 15 days.

Type in the seller's eBay ID, click the 'Include completed listings' box and all the current listings that ended in the period you choose (one day, seven days and 15 days) will be displayed. Leave this box empty and all current listings will be shown. Fig 5 shows the page for searching for items by seller.

Use Find items > By seller search to see how the market is performing for other sellers. If your competitors are selling the same items as you hope to, consider holding back for a while.

Fig 5. Find items by seller

Advanced search

Items	Items by seller
Find items	**Enter seller's user ID**
By seller	
By bidder	
By item number	Find items offered by a particular seller.
Shop	☐ Show completed listings only `Last 15 days ↕`
	☐ Show close and exact user ID matches
Items in Shops	
Find Shops	**Sort by:**
	`Best Match ↕`
Members	**Results per page**
Find a member	`50 ↕`
Find contact information	
Find a Trading Assistant	**Search**

3. Find items > By bidder

In the same way as the above search, it is also possible to search for the items that a particular user is bidding on. You can also select the items that they bid on during the last month. As a seller you may need to discover if a bidder is serious about your item. Are they an avid collector with a track record of purchases in this area?

This search will also show if the bidder went on to win the item and who the seller is.

 Use this search to track your competitors' buying activity. If they buy and sell through the same ID, you can see if they have found an item of interest and perhaps go on to bid against them and win the item yourself. You are letting other people do your research for you – follow their bidding activity and then outbid them at the last minute.

Where to find stock

The most closely guarded secret of all salespeople is where they obtain their stock. Nobody who trades on eBay, or anywhere else, will advise of their stock supplier. If you manufacture your own items, or have an existing supplier relationship, then stick with what you know. If you do not have such an arrangement this section may give some insight into a few areas that might just lead to a source of goods to sell.

Possible sources are:

1. Traditional wholesalers.

2. eBay.

3. Other internet sources.

4. Traditional auctions.

5. Second-hand items.

6. Retail outlets.

7. Drop-shipping.

8. Market traders.

These are explained below.

1. Traditional wholesalers

If you know the kind of thing that you would like to sell, you should be able to find a wholesaler who can supply the items. Check your local press and the internet. It is possible to buy lists of wholesalers that have been compiled by a third party. For a few pounds, this option may save you time trawling through the internet.

If you have never dealt with a wholesaler before, you may find the experience is not exactly as you would expect. Here are a few things to consider:

• Prices will not include VAT. Ensure that you factor this into any price calculations when working through your margins. Expect to pay 20% (the current rate of VAT in the UK) more than the published price.

• Check for minimum order values. Ask about order sizes and consider the impact on your cash flow and storage. Do not underestimate how much room you will need.

• Are they genuine brands? Ask for a sample before placing a big order.

• Prices do not include carriage. Check how much it will cost to have the items delivered to you.

- You may have to provide references. Some wholesalers will require references from your current business contacts and there is bound to be a form to fill in.

- Mixed lots. As some manufacturers pack similar lines in the same box, be prepared for a delivery that has almost what you asked for. The quantity will be correct, but the particular items may vary each time.

- Be bold. Your wholesaler will also supply to other traders. If they have something you like that sells well and is at the right price, buy as much as you can – it may all be gone when you want to re-order.

- Cash or account? There are two ways to pay for your goods: cash or on account. If you want to open an account, be prepared to fill in more forms and provide bank details.

- Will the item sell? Wholesalers often have remainder lines that would not sell in retail outlets; can you sell them? Before placing a large order, do your research, check other sellers on eBay and see if there is a market for the product.

- Is there enough margin? Use eBay listings as a benchmark for achievable prices. Check completed and active listings and see what the item actually sold for. (Read Chapter 3 of this book for more search tips.) Unsold items may give you some indication as to the prices that could not be achieved.

Wholesalers acquire a variety of goods from bankrupt companies. These may sound great and be well priced, but remember the previous owner of them didn't fare too well.

2. eBay

eBay is a great place to buy goods for resale. Once you have mastered all the elements of this book, you will understand for your own area what sells and for what price. Check eBay for sellers who do not know the value of their items, buy them cheaply and resell them in a more professional way.

Look for sellers who:

- Trade only with the UK. These sellers have severely restricted their marketplace and their items will not reach high sale prices.

- Insist on collection only. Not posting an item will restrict prices and should allow you to pick up a bargain if you live locally.

- Have made mistakes in the description of their item. Maybe the spelling of a keyword is wrong; if so, fewer bidders will find the listing.

- List auctions that end in the early hours of the morning. If nobody is awake then they can't bid and prices should remain lower.

 If you find an auction with a mistake in the title, make a small bid. Once a bid has been placed, the seller cannot revise the title, therefore locking the mistake in and restricting the number of competitors you will have for the item.

Use these techniques and you will be able to pick up stock at a reasonable price. You can then sell it on to a global market in a professional way, and you should see an increase on the price that you paid for it.

Sum of the parts...

Consider buying collections of items and splitting them down into more manageable lots. This will involve a higher purchase price but the sum of the parts should be more than the entire collection, as individual items will appeal to more bidders with less money to spend.

I still buy large collections of Thomas the Tank Engine items this way and then add the pieces on to my 'multi-variation' listing and just wait for them to sell. There is a likelihood that you will not sell everything quickly so be aware of your cash flow situation.

Use the eBay search facility (see Chapter 3) to check for some of these keywords:

- Massive.

- Huge.

- Collection.

- Lots.

- Loads.

- Wholesale.

Remember that large collections of items will weigh a lot; these will cost more to post and are more difficult to send overseas. This is just the type of listing you should be looking for.

Buy Lego by weight, CDs by collections, and mobile phone car kits; then split these large lots into component parts.

To move ahead of other eBay users using these methods to buy stock, use the advanced search facility and search for your item using:

- Buy It Now as a purchase option. This will allow you to obtain stock that much quicker and remove the item from circulation.

- Listings started within 1 hour – you will be one of the first people to see the item and if it suits your needs, buy it immediately.

 When you find an auction that looks promising, place a bid there and then. Too many times I have forgotten to check back and missed the auction end. The proxy bidding system will bid on your behalf up to your maximum amount, so just enter the amount you're prepared to pay and hope no one else finds the same auction.

Wholesale & job lots

There is also another great place to buy large volumes of stock on eBay – the Wholesale category. Access this in the same way as any other: go to the eBay home page, use the drop-down menu at the top of the page, scroll to the bottom of the list and click 'Wholesale & Job Lots'. There will be something here for most eBay traders.

 Keep the packaging that your purchases arrive in, if it is still in good condition. You may well be able to re-use it for your own sales and save some money.

3. Other internet sources

eBay is not the only auction site on the internet, although it is by far the biggest. Depending on the type of items you intend to sell, you may be able to buy from one site and sell on another. Items for sale on other auction sites might not get as many visitors as eBay, so there may be a discount on prices.

Below I have listed some of the other main sites. Check them out; you never know what you might find:

- eBid (uk.ebid.net).

- Freecycle (uk.freecycle.org).

- uBid (www.ubid.com).

- Gumtree (www.gumtree.com).

4. Traditional auctions

The traditional, non-cyber auction house may also be a place to obtain stock. In a traditional auction items will usually sell to somebody in the room, and on certain days there may not be many people present. Bid wisely, pick up a bargain, list it on eBay and sell to a global market.

General auctions are exactly what you would expect, an assortment of lots to pick and choose from. Specialist auctions might be of more interest; however, at specialist toy auctions I am always outbid by collectors.

You can usually view all the lots the day before an auction or for a short time on the actual day.

There are a few things to consider if you are new to auction houses, these include:

- Stay away from the tea and coffee. This is time to do business.

- Wrap up warm during the winter months as these places can be cold.

- Be prepared to pay a buyer's premium of around 15% + VAT. This will be added to your 'hammer price'.

- Ensure you check any potential purchases carefully; things are not always what they seem.

- You may need to provide proof of identity when you register, so take along your driving licence.

- Paying with cash is the easiest way; cheques can be troublesome and credit cards attract an additional fee.

Amongst what was fundamentally a load of junk I once spotted a used-stamp album which I picked up for £28. Inside were £87 of unfranked UK stamps, which I put to good use shipping out my eBay items to buyers.

5. Second-hand items

The second-hand market always has bargains to be found. Consider your local newspaper adverts, car boot sales, charity shops and so on. Once you have accumulated some knowledge of eBay and have an understanding of prices that can be obtained, you will know if a particular item could yield a profit.

When considering second-hand items for resale, there are a few things to be aware of before you make your purchase.

- Consider the condition of older items. Of course, the wear and tear may be part of the item's appeal; the whole antiques market is, after all, just second-hand goods.

- Think about how much time will be needed to prepare the item for sale – is there just too much work involved?

Spare parts market

Used items can be a great source of spares for other models. If you are intending to sell model trains, for example, then you will need a selection of spare parts. There is a market for well-priced used spares for all kinds of items, including toys, electrical items, computers and domestic appliances.

Having changed our family vacuum cleaner, I was left with an old Dyson upright cleaner, still serviceable, if a little noisy. This was much too heavy for me to sell on eBay; I just don't have the packing materials. So I dismantled the machine and sold the attachments, hose, electric switches and even the power cable.

When selling replacement parts, offer them for instant purchase with Buy It Now. If an item has broken, the buyer will not want to wait a week to get the replacement part.

Second-hand items to avoid

Some things can look like a bargain but can prove to be just too much hard work. If you do sell something that is faulty, putting it right can be costly as well as time consuming. The list below includes just some of the things I would avoid when looking for used items.

- Technology which could well be out of date or out of vogue.
- Computer software which may not work on all types of computer.
- Jigsaws or Lego sets which might have parts missing.
- Electrical items that you cannot see working.

 If you are a car boot sale fan and buy items to sell on eBay, don't discard all the junk that may come with your purchase. Instead put it to one side and enter it into a general sale at a traditional auction house – you will be amazed at what people will buy. I use these for 'Mega-Bloks', broken toys, incomplete games, heavy wooden toys and so on.

6. Retail outlets

It is even possible to buy stock from the high street and sell it for a profit. Old lines, discontinued stock and even sale items may well not be available overseas. Certain toys, for example, are not sold throughout the world, so a particular model in the UK may not be available elsewhere. Know your market and you will be able to make money in this way.

High street stores report their sales and profit figures quarterly and will often have sales just before these deadlines. The period between Christmas and New Year has traditionally been very good for me with many major chains reducing prices of stock.

I now have such a good relationship with some high street stores that I get Boxing Day discounts on Christmas Eve. Well, nobody really wants to get up early on 26 December do they? Discounts of 30% to 50% are fairly common.

The Boots 75% sale is always a good source of bargains, check it out in mid-January. Debenhams often reduce Christmas lines by up to 70% with extra 10% days and vouchers in the press.

Children's fancy dress costumes are always reduced after Christmas; I buy these and hold them until Halloween. And it is not just the scary outfits that are in demand. After Halloween I go back into the shops and buy what they didn't sell with the best deals coming from QD Stores, with costumes and accessories for just 10p each.

Stores where I have found great sale bargains are M&S, TKMaxx, Boots and Debenhams. My strategy is to drink as much coffee as possible and check out the sale section as I pass by.

 In my early days on eBay, I bought Arsenal Monopoly for £24.99 in Woolworths and then sold it on eBay the same day for £45. I enjoyed that so much I did it six more times!

7. Drop-shipping

Have you ever wanted to sell something on eBay but never handle it, not have to pack it for dispatch and not have to pay for it up front – but still pocket the profit? Well, drop shipping may be for you.

Here's how it works:

- You open an eBay seller's account.
- You find a supplier who is willing to supply you with the products you want to sell.
- You establish an account as a retailer, with the supplier you choose.
- You receive images and descriptions of the products you want to sell from the supplier and use these in your eBay listings.
- If priced correctly and all the other aspects of your eBay business are in order, your item will sell.
- You send the buyer's details to your supplier.
- The wholesale supplier sends the product directly to your customer, with your details included; the buyer will not know that a third party was involved with the delivery.
- You then pay the supplier for the item and the delivery charge, and retain any margin between the buying and selling price.
- Your buyer receives the item and leaves you great feedback.

Advantages:

- No outlay for stock.

- Sell before you buy.

- No packing (what a result, I hate packing!)

Potential problems:

- Your supplier represents you in the area of packing and dispatch; if they get it wrong, you will get the blame.

- Selecting the right supplier; trust is a key element in this business, start with something small and test their abilities.

Does it all sound too good to be true? Well, in my opinion yes. Judging from the number of readers who contact me concerning their experiences in this area I would advise great caution if you are considering this approach. If it was that easy, everybody would be doing it.

8. Market traders

Make friends with your local market traders as these guys often have lines that can be sold on eBay. Cash talks in this world and if you offer them a good price for the entirety of their stock you can often cut a deal.

Some of my best deals have been from friendly market stall holders including a nice line in puppy raincoats and a huge quantity of DeWalt drill bits that made me a fortune. Perhaps the most unusual deal was for 15,000 empty bags in an assortment of designs. These sold extremely well on eBay to other sellers who filled them full of goodies for Christmas; I ended up being the wholesaler!

Where I found my wholesalers

Obtaining stock at the right price can be the biggest hurdle to a successful eBay business and it's the one area that sellers are reluctant to discuss. Teaming up with a reliable wholesaler is essential if you want to grow your business and ensure you never run out of things to sell. But where do you start?

eSources (www.eSources.co.uk) is the largest directory of UK wholesale distributors, suppliers and products. If you are looking for stock, these guys certainly know enough wholesalers and could be just what you need. Soon after embarking on my eBay career I subscribed to eSources and found two great wholesalers who I still use to this day. It must be said that I did also have to wade through a lot of non-starters as well; it does take some time to find the perfect partner.

When to sell

When you sell on eBay will probably depend upon your other commitments. If you sell frequently, your cash flow will improve as you will turn your stock around more frequently. If you sell less often but list a number of auctions at a time then you must expect a very busy time when the listings end.

How long you let your auction listings run may well depend on how quickly you need to sell. If your old three piece suite is still in the lounge after delivery of the new one then a shorter duration auction is probably a good idea [Ed: this sounds like the voice of experience].

If you go down the Buy It Now route then timing is less of an issue as the listing just keeps going until all items are sold or the listing expires. You can get around the admin involved with managing expiring listings with a shop – more on this later. With BIN listings sales will occur on an ad hoc basis, but usually more in the first week of the month, soon after payday.

How much time does eBay take?

One of the most attractive aspects of running a business on eBay is the choice you have to work as little or as much as you like. There are, of course, some restrictions. There are only so many hours in the day and the stock you sell may run out, limiting the work you can do. But, as a general rule, the more time you spend selling on eBay, the more money you will make.

The number of listings that you have on eBay will depend on your own circumstances. However, the greater the volume, the more work it will take to manage them. As a guide, I find my time spent on different activities divides roughly as follows:

- Preparing items (photographing, writing descriptions and uploading) – 20%

- Packing and posting – 30%

- Research – 10%

- After sales paperwork – 10%

- Admin – 10%

- Sourcing products – 20%

As I now have three distinctly different stock lines the amount of time on each does vary. Packing lipsticks in bubble bags does not take that long and a couple of hours each day is more than enough. My range of DIY and electrical items also don't need much work to pack and send. But toys come in a variety of shapes and need a little more thought when packing; it is this side of the business which takes the time.

Now that I have a finely tuned process in place for all my product lines I can get away with a working week of around 20 hours, most of which is on a Sunday during car boot season and on a Monday catching up with weekend sales.

Seasonal trading

Just as retail outlets on the high street will change their range according to the season, you may decide to do the same. Toys and gifts will sell better at Christmas, and clothes should be sold according to the season. Collectables and regularly used items such as batteries seem to have a steady market all year round.

Sales tend to trail off during the hot summer months as people spend less time in front of their computers and more time in the garden. During this period it would be advisable to start auctions at the minimum price you would expect as you may get fewer bids to push prices higher.

During the summer months I alter my sales strategy, focusing more on collectables and DIY items. Cosmetic staples such as creams and lotions sell throughout the year, gift sets I hold until Christmas. I save my main stock of toys for the Christmas rush, which starts in late September, but save construction toys such as Meccano and K'Nex until January when the nights are longer and kids play indoors.

As a general rule, sell things during the summer months that are likely to be used by the buyer themselves. Items such as replacement parts, collectables, spares for domestic appliances, and so on. During the run up to Christmas, sell things that may be purchased as gifts for someone else.

Christmas trading

The Christmas trading period deserves a special mention as it is something you have to experience to believe. I have now completed nine Christmases and each year I start preparing in June. To say things get hectic is an understatement and that anything you put up for sale will sell and make crazy money is… probably right!

After the summer slump when bidders are on the beach or outside with the BBQ comes the realisation that Christmas is only a few weeks away. When the children go back to school in September, something happens to the nation's buyers; they seem to enter a frenzy. Even – perhaps especially – during a recession the Christmas period is by far the busiest time of the year.

If you are selling overseas and sending items by surface post, then the last day for sending them is somewhere around mid-October, so you will get overseas interest in September as well.

 Work hard in the run up to Christmas, don't sleep at all, and then take it easy for the next three months.

How to cope with the rush

There are a few things you can do in the anticipation of high sales during the Christmas period:

- Prepare your inventory of items, stock up well and tailor your items towards Christmas presents. Put away the Dyson spares and find the Lego sets.

- Take as many pictures as you can during the summer when times are quieter and the natural light is better. Store these away on your computer.

- Stock up on packaging materials well in advance. My output trebles at this time of year, so having enough boxes and bubble wrap is essential.

- Anticipate the time it will take to complete the packing and listing. Don't undertake major home improvements, or other activities that will be a draw on your time, in this period. You may need to take time off work (if you still have a 'day' job) if things get really manic.

- Recruit additional help – rope the family into some packing duties. Hard-up students in your family are always a good prospect and easy to exploit.

Frequency of trading

Your commitments may mean that you can only list items once a week, or even once a month, or you may choose to list items every day. Each approach has its own advantages and disadvantages. Trial and error will help you find the best policy for your particular lifestyle. I tend to list a few items every day, this keeps my shop well stocked whilst not becoming too boring a task.

I try to maintain a stock level in the cosmetics shop of around 200 lines, while the DIY/toy shop has around 1,400 items active at any one time.

Establish your selling account

Once you have an idea of what you would like to sell and when, it is time to create your eBay selling account.

You may already have an eBay account as a buyer, you may already sell on eBay, or eBay may be completely new to you. This section will look in more detail at choosing a username, the types of account available and how to set up a seller's account from the beginning.

 I have several eBay accounts, including one for buying, one for the sale of personal items and my main ID – Mollybol – which is an eBay shop and used to sell my range of cosmetics. The toy and DIY business share a shop at the moment but will be split in the future.

Your eBay ID

Selecting your eBay ID is the hardest part of the registration process, as most of the names you think of will have already been taken. It is, however, the most vital element – creating a trading name that meets the following criteria should ensure greater sales success:

- **Name length**. When a buyer wants to search for you by name, maybe just to browse your items, they will need to type your name into the search engines. The longer your name, the more likely they are to make a mistake when typing and never reach your items at all. Keep it short!

- **Format**. Keep the format easy to type: hyphens are often forgotten; underscores require two keys to be pressed; and numbers are awkward to remember.

- **Memorable**. Make your name memorable. Try to construct a name that can be pronounced – the most obvious names have been taken, but with some thought you should be able to arrive at something. A jumble of letters and numbers, maybe initials and a date of birth, such as BGH121070, will not be remembered. The idea is to encourage as many satisfied customers as possible to come back to buy again.

- **Relevant**. If you intend to focus on a specific area of sales, try to make your name relevant to the market. You may already have found some sellers who have the item they sell within their name – examples might include Nokiaman, Batteryseller, DVDshop and so on. (I have just made these up to illustrate how a name can reflect the sales activity.)

The beginning of a brand

Your trading name will form the beginning of your brand identity. Changing it at a later date is possible, but should be avoided to ensure that your existing customers don't lose track of you. You may decide to incorporate your name on to stationery, packing slips, address labels, email signatures, etc. You may even advertise in the future.

My main trading ID is 'Mollybol'. Molly is the name of the family dog and the 'bol' relates to a word commonly used after hitting the wrong key on your computer and losing all your work! [Ed: hopefully there weren't too many 'bol' moments in the writing of this book.]

Top five things to consider when choosing a name

1. **Keep it short**. Make your name easy for visitors to type. Don't make them rewrite *War and Peace* just to find you.

2. **Only use letters**. Avoid using numbers in your name; letters are easier to remember.

3. **Use a real word**. Make your name into something that can be pronounced; a jumble of letters won't be remembered.

4. **Avoid current trends**. Choose a name that won't date. Avoid topical films and other subjects that won't mean as much in a few years' time.

5. **Consider more than one account**. Establish separate accounts for each product area you sell in and maybe another as a buying account. This allows your name to be relevant to what you are selling.

Creating an account

Having chosen a trading name, the next stage is to set up a trading account on eBay. You may choose to create a new selling account or use an existing account.

Creating a new selling account

The process for creating a selling account is very straightforward:

- If you already have an account as a buyer, simply upgrade from your My eBay section.

- If you are starting from scratch, go to the eBay home page and click on 'register' in the top left of the screen. Fig 6 shows the registration page.

Fig 6. Registration page

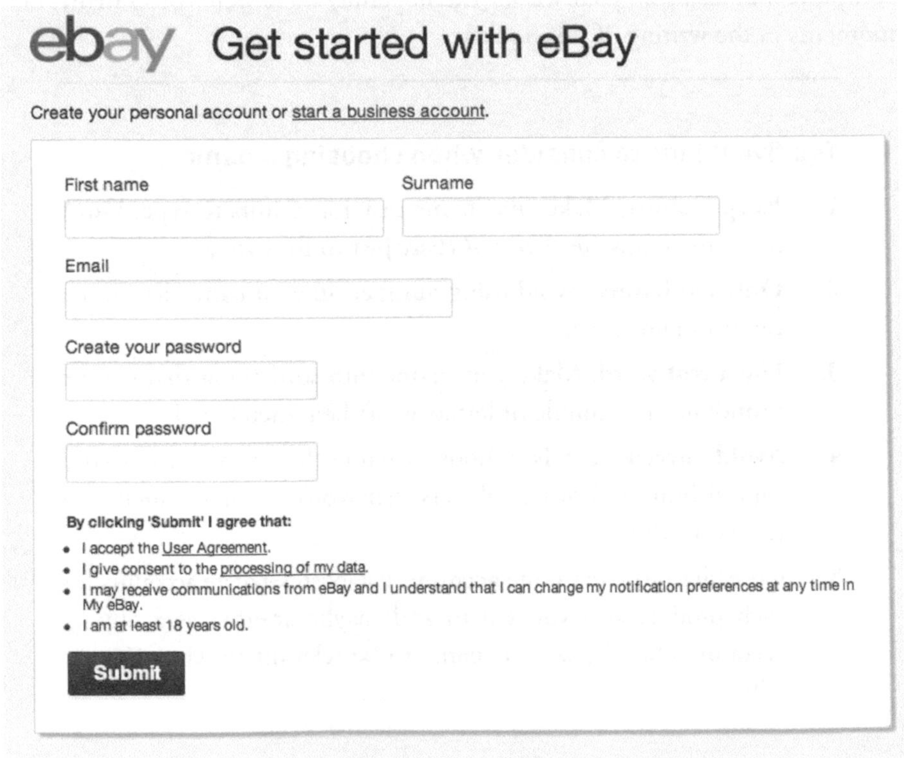

ebay Get started with eBay

Create your personal account or start a business account.

First name

Surname

Email

Create your password

Confirm password

By clicking 'Submit' I agree that:

- I accept the User Agreement.
- I give consent to the processing of my data.
- I may receive communications from eBay and I understand that I can change my notification preferences at any time in My eBay.
- I am at least 18 years old.

Submit

The instructions are easy to follow. You will need to enter your personal contact details, email address and so on. eBay will first create an account for you as a buyer, which you can then upgrade to a seller's account.

When setting up as a seller you will be asked for a credit card number or your bank account details, or both. This is to ensure that eBay can collect their fees when you create your first listing or make your first sale. You will only have to enter these once. There are no upfront charges and you will not need to deposit any money with eBay.

If you are starting with a new account, consider buying a few low-priced items from this account to get started. This will boost your feedback score and also give you an insight into the buyer's point of view, which will be helpful when selling your own items.

You can monitor your account status and see how much money you owe eBay in fees by clicking on the 'Account' link on the My eBay page and then clicking on 'Fees' at any time. (Fees are discussed in much more detail in a later section.)

Using an existing account

You can of course use an existing account to sell through, as well as buy with. This can be a good idea if you already have a high feedback score, as some selling facilities only become available with a certain number of successful trades. If your feedback as a buyer is not that good, create a new account and start afresh.

Ensure that you have your correct address details saved on both eBay and PayPal as sellers can use either site to find the address to send your parcel to.

If you're selling and buying on eBay

Give some thought as to where you may acquire stock in the future. If you intend to buy from eBay and then sell it back via eBay (something I will look at later in greater detail), a separate buyer's account might be a good idea. This will avoid the situation where your buying and selling activity can be viewed within the same account. For one thing, it might upset the person you bought the items from to see them turned around and sold on for a healthy profit.

Consider renaming your account. Perhaps the single most important aspect to successful eBay selling is the name that you trade with. It is your brand identity and the name that bidders will search for if they want to come back to you in the future to buy again.

To change your eBay ID:

1. Go to My eBay > Account > Personal information.

2. Click Edit to the far right of your User ID.

Private account vs business account

If like me you begin by selling your own items and then progress to selling items bought for resale, then upgrading to a business account is required. It might be tempting to remain as a private seller and 'hide' your eBay activities. However, for the sake of a peaceful night take the plunge and upgrade to business. There are a few more requirements – such as the need to have a returns policy – but there are a few advantages as well.

Advantages of a business account

- Business sellers can register with a company name. That company name will be displayed in all communication with the buyer, such as invoices and emails.
- Business sellers could be eligible to qualify for a discount on eBay fees.
- Business sellers can display contact details and terms and conditions in all of their listings.
- Business sellers could realise tax advantages if they register as a business.

Choose your target market

One of the biggest decisions when selling on eBay is to choose how large you would like your target market to be. The world is a very big and complicated place – particularly in respect of foreign business markets – and it is much more comfortable to sell only to the UK as it is a place you know.

There are some things that you would not want to sell overseas. These might include items that are too heavy, too valuable (in case of the item being lost in transit – when I say lost I mean stolen), too tricky to pack, or where the hidden cost of shipping is too high (this refers to the fees charged by eBay on postage charges and a fee levied by PayPal which increases with higher shipping costs).

Overview of the eBay selling zones

eBay will let you choose your marketplace. There is a comprehensive set of options for what countries an item will be available to during the listing process and you can change your options for different items. The pros and cons of the various marketplaces are listed below.

UK only

Advantages

- The UK is a familiar place.
- No language concerns.
- Next-day delivery is possible.
- You can agree local pickup or delivery.
- Weight and packing considerations are well known.

Within the UK the postage costs are very clear and you should be familiar with the way the Post Office works. You understand the way that parcels should be sent and even the regular updates for parcel pricing are workable once you get to grips with the small print. Sending mail overseas is something that you may not have done before.

Disadvantages

- A limited market.
- More competition from UK-only sellers.
- Sale price may be compromised.

There is no doubt that if an item is available to a larger audience it will attract more attention, so you could get more sales.

Europe

Advantages

- Larger potential customer base than just the UK.
- Fewer customs restrictions than trading worldwide.

Disadvantages

- Weight and packing requirements are different.
- Delivery time (air mail/surface mail).
- Currency considerations (not always the euro).
- Language considerations.

Sell to as much of the world as you feel comfortable with. Make your potential market as big as possible – it is as straightforward as that.

Global

Advantages

- The largest marketplace currently available (assuming the moon is not colonised before you read this).

Disadvantages

- Customs clearance.
- Shipping requirements and insurance.
- Payment options are limited – these buyers will almost certainly only be able to pay you by PayPal.
- Multiple currency options.
- Language considerations.
- Returns are more complicated.

What to consider when choosing your target market

When choosing your marketplace it is important to conduct extensive research and market your products accordingly. How you actually design your eBay pages to address this will depend on the product and the countries you wish to sell into. Here are just a few areas which may well be worth considering early on:

- **The weight of your items**. The more your item weighs, the higher the postage charges will be. This may make it too expensive for overseas buyers, and will restrict your market and profit margin. Remember that both eBay and PayPal will take their share.

- **Operating and legal restrictions**. Some countries will have different restrictions on what can be sent. If you intend to market a particular product overseas, check to see if it is permitted for import into the country you intend to sell to.

- **UK shipping regulations.** What can and cannot be shipped will change, so you have to keep abreast of this. For example, it is now very difficult to send perfume within the UK using the Royal Mail and it is prohibited to send any overseas.

- **Time delays.** Shipping outside of the UK will take longer and this may have a negative impact on your feedback scores as frustrated buyers blame you for delayed delivery. This is likely to be compounded in the run up to Christmas.

 The first item I sold outside of the UK was a music CD to Canada. It happened by accident. At the time I was only selling in the UK and had no idea of what would be involved in shipping worldwide. But the highest bidder was in Canada, so I had to learn the process at the end of the auction or lose the sale.

---

eBay fees

When managing any retail business it is important to make a profit as a reward for your time and effort, and so you can afford to live. This means you need to make enough money to cover your expenses.

In a later section we will look more closely at bookkeeping but for now give some thought to the amount of money you want as a wage. Understanding the fee structure of eBay will help you determine if the items you have in mind to sell will actually be worth the trouble and whether you stand to make any money.

Fee structure

eBay is constantly changing its pricing structure. Here I can only give guidance and comment on the fee structure at the time of writing, so please check the information on screen for the fees payable when you actually list an item.

Just to make things more complex, the fees may differ depending on whether you are a private seller or a business seller, so consider how you will run things and which fees will apply to you.

The fee structure at the time of writing for either an auction or BIN listing is basically split into three parts:

1. Insertion fee.

2. Final value fee.

3. Optional feature fees.

1. Insertion fee

Auctions

You will be charged a fee to place your listing on eBay unless you are a private seller and select the auction format starting at 99p or less – this is now free for the first 20 listings.

Table 1 shows insertion fees for business sellers.

Table 1. Insertion fees (business sellers)

			Insertion fees			
Approx. listings per month	Shop level	Monthly subscription	Free fixed-price listings	Price per additional fixed-price listing	Price per auction starting under £1	Price per auction starting at £1 or more
Up to 65	None	Free	0	£0.30	£0.10	£0.30
65–600	Basic	£19.99	200	£0.10	£0.05	£0.15
600–5000	Featured	£59.99	1200	£0.05	£0.05	£0.15
Over 5000	Anchor	£249.99	Unlimited	Free	£0.05	£0.15

Buy It Now listings

For standard BIN listings the insertion fee will be a flat 30p irrespective of how many items you include within the listing or the total value of the items. Things get more complicated with BIN items if you have an eBay shop – as you can see in Table 1, the insertion fee will vary depending upon the type of shop you have (more about eBay shops later in the book).

You can see from this table why I keep my cosmetic shop stocked at 200 lines. With a basic shop I pay a £19.99 fee but get 200 listings included which, at 10p per listing, is my shop subscription back.

I understand that eBay are considering a move away from up-front listing costs towards a success-based charging system which will allow sellers to list for free and then charge a higher fee when the item sells. Amazon already has this fee structure in place, but charge sellers a much higher percentage final fee than eBay. eBay has started to introduce this policy with the inclusive allowance of free listings within the costs of operating an eBay shop (as shown in Table 1).

Notes on BIN listing fees

- All listings must start at £0.99 or more. Sellers are not permitted to start a listing in Buy It Now format for under £0.99.

- If your item does not sell or if your buyer does not pay, you will not be eligible to get a re-list credit for your insertion fees.

- You pay the same insertion fee to list multiple identical items in the one listing as you would to list an individual item. For example, say the insertion fee payable for listing one item is £0.30. If you list four identical items in one listing, the insertion fee charged is the same (£0.30).

- It is possible to list your items in a format known as a multi-variation listing (MVL). This is one listing with similar yet slightly different items, maybe the same shirt but in a number of sizes and colours. This is ideal for my electrical fuse listings where I have the same manufacturer with several different amperages. More on the MVL later.

Consdering the implications of insertion fees

If you sell books, CDs or DVDs in the media category, for example, the insertion fee will be 10p if you are a business seller and start an auction below

£1. This is obviously lower than the flat 20p insertion fee you would pay to list this item as BIN. However, once you start the auction at more than £1 it is more cost effective to list the item as Buy It Now than as an auction. Choosing the right way to list your items is key to the profitability of your business.

2. Final value fee (FVF)

eBay will then also charge a percentage of the final sale price of an item including postage charge, packaging and any other costs. That is to say the fee is on the total amount the buyer pays you. This is referred to as the final value fee (FVF).

As with insertion fees, FVFs differ depending on whether you are a private or business seller, whether you use auction or BIN, and the final value the item is sold for. Also, media and technology categories attract different FVFs to those of other categories. The majority of FVFs are shown in Table 2.

As you can see, it is important to place your listing within the right category. If your item legitimately fits into more than one category then you clearly need to be listing it in the category for which you will pay the lowest fees. This can save you loads in fees in the long run.

Table 2. Final value fees by category (business sellers)

Category	Final value fee	Exceptions
Antiques	10%	None
Art	10%	None
Baby	10%	None
Books, Comics & Magazines	9%	None
Business, Office & Industrial	11%	None
Cameras & Photography	8%	5% final value fee (max. £10) for: - Lenses & Filters - Camcorders - Digital Cameras
Clothes, Shoes & Accessories	11%	None
Coins	10%	None
Collectables	9%	None

Computers, Tablets & Networking	8%	5% final value fee (max. £10) for: - Desktops & All-in-ones - Drives, Storage & Blank Media - iPads/Tablets & eBook Readers - Laptops & Netbooks - Printers, Scanners & Suppliers - Software - Wireless Routers
Crafts	11%	None
Dolls & Bears	11%	None
DVDs, Films & TV	9%	None
Event Tickets	11%	10% final value fee (max. £10) for: - Gift Vouchers & Coupons
Garden & Patio	10%	None
Health & Beauty	10%	None
Holidays & Travel	10% (max £40)	None
Home, Furniture & DIY	11%	5% final value fee (max.£10) for: - Appliances - Power Tools 10% final value fee (max. £40) for: - Furniture - Bath
Jewellery & Watches	11%	11% final value fee (max. £50) for: - Watches
Mobile Phones & Communication	8%	5% final value fee (max. £10) for: - Home Phones & Accessories - Mobile & Smart Phones
Music	9%	None
Musical Instruments	10%	None
Pet Supplies	11%	None
Pottery, Porcelain & Glass	11%	None
Sound & Vision	8%	5% final value fee to a max. of £10 for: - DVD, Blu-ray & Home Cinema - Headphones - Home Audio & HiFi Separates - iPods & MP3 Players - Televisions - TV Reception & Set-top Boxes
Sporting Goods	10% (max £50)	None
Sports Memorabilia	10%	None
Stamps	10%	None
Toys & Games	10%	None

Vehicle Parts & Accessories	8%	6% final value fee (max. £15) for: - Tyres - Tyres & Tubes 5% final value fee (max. £10) for: - GPS & Sat Nav - Power Tools & Equipment
Video Games & Consoles	9%	5% final value fee (max. £10) for: - Consoles
Wholesale & Job Lots	11%	9% final value fee for: - PC & Video Gaming
Everything Else	11%	None

When you sell your item using the auction format as a private seller, you will pay a maximum of 10% of the item's final selling price as the final value fee, up to a maximum of £75. If the item does not sell, there is no final value fee.

 One good thing about the most recent fee changes is the introduction of a maximum fee payable. It doesn't help me at all though as all my items sell well below the £750 break-even point for this.

3. Optional feature fees

eBay will also offer you some optional upgrades to your basic listing design. I will expand on these services when we look in more detail about the listing procedure itself, but for now they are important to consider in terms of the costs of running your eBay business.

Below I give more information about these fees.

Listing upgrade fees

You can enhance your listing by adding various features, such as a subtitle, Gallery Plus and a BIN option. Table 3 provides a summary of these fees.

Table 3. Listing upgrade fees

Optional listing upgrade	Price per listing
Gallery Plus*	£2.50
Adding Buy It Now to auctions	£0.50
Subtitle	£1.00
Listing designer**	£0.30

Notes:
*Gallery Plus is free if you sell in Fashion, Motors, Home and Garden or Pet Supplies.
**Listing Designer is free for all selling tools; more on these tools later.

Setting a reserve price

You can choose the minimum you're willing to sell your item for. If you set a reserve price of £50 or more, you'll pay 4% of that price as a fee. You'll never pay a reserve fee of more than £150 per item.

Picture service fees

Great news: all pictures are now free. Yippee!!

This means you can have 12 pictures of each item for free in all categories. It works for me with toys and some DIY products as I can now load close-up pictures into the gallery on my listings. There are still some benefits of loading pictures into your description using HTML and I will cover these later.

It gets even better if you opt for the 'Multi-variation' listing format and fully load it with 60 items as each item can have 12 pictures. This means you could have 720 pictures on one listing, all for free; now that's value for money!

International site visibility

This will place your item into the default search results of other international eBay sites. In theory this should give your item better exposure and increase the chance of a sale overseas. This option is currently only available for Australia, the USA and Canada; more sites are likely to be included in the future. The fees are shown in Table 4.

Table 4. International site visibility fees

Starting price	Auction-style fee	Buy It Now fee (all durations)
£0.01 – £4.99	£0.05	£0.30
£5.00 – £29.99	£0.10	£0.30
£30+	£0.15	£0.30

Examples of eBay fees for private sellers

To provide an example of eBay fees for a private seller, let's say you are listing a media-related item using the auction-style format.

- Starting price: £50.
- Final selling price: £150.
- Postage & Packaging cost: £10.
- Total eBay selling fees are £16.10 comprising:
  - Insertion fee: £0.10.
  - Final value fee: 10% of the total cost including postage, packaging and any other related costs, which in this case is £16.

If you listed an item using the free auction-style listing:

- Starting price: £0.99.
- Final selling price: £25.
- Postage & Packaging cost: £2.
- Total eBay selling fees are £2.70 comprising:
  - Insertion fee: £0.
  - Final value fee: 10% of the total cost including postage, packaging and any other related costs, which in this case is £2.70.

If you listed a technology-related item using the Buy It Now format:

- Buy It Now price: £30.
- Final selling price: £30.
- Postage & Packaging cost: £5.
- Total eBay selling fees are £3.90 comprising:
  - Insertion fee: £0.40.
  - Final value fee: 10% of the total cost including postage, packaging and any other related costs, which in this case is £3.50.

If listing an item using the auction-style format with a reserve price:

- Starting price: £10.

- Reserve price: £150.

- Final selling price: £200.

- Postage & Packaging cost: £10

- Total eBay selling fees are £28.30 comprising:

  - Insertion fee: £1.30.

  - Reserve fee: 4% of the reserve price, which in this case is £6.

  - Final value fee: 10% of the total cost including postage, packaging and any other related costs, which in this case is £21.

Top-rated seller discount scheme

You will no doubt see the Top-rated seller (TRS) programme advertised as you move around the eBay site.

If you see a listing which states that the seller provides "eBay premium service" then that seller is part of the TRS programme. eBay says:

> "eBay Top-rated sellers are PowerSellers who consistently provide the best buying experiences to their customers. Whether you have a large volume of sales or smaller volume of a higher value, you can be a Top-rated seller."

I say:

> "This is a discount scheme which will reward high-volume sellers who are registered as a business. As long as you keep your account in good standing, meet the postage and dispatch criteria, offer exceptional customer service and achieve a certain sales figure you will get a discount on your final value fee for any listing that meets the 'eBay premium service' requirements. (There is no discount on insertion fees.)"

The implementation of the scheme has been, to say the least, problematic and controversial. At various points the discounts offered have been 40%, 30% and now they stand at 15% (can you see the pattern here?). The qualifying criteria have also become more demanding with time, so fewer sellers enjoy smaller discounts. Oh well.

Qualifying as a TRS

To qualify as a Top-rated seller you will need to achieve a certain level of performance measured against a raft of criteria which seem to change every six months or so. Table 5 lays out the numbers you need to be aware of. It is interesting to note that all sellers must achieve a minimum standard or face exclusion, I'll delve into this in more detail later.

Table 5. Top-rated seller requirements

Requirement	Minimum for all sellers	eBay Top-rated sellers
Defect rate		
Maximum percentage of transactions with defects	5%	2%
Minimum number of unique buyers affected before seller status is impacted	8	5
Closed cases without seller resolution		
Maximum percentage of cases closed by eBay without seller resolution	0.3% or no more than 2	0.3% or no more than 2
Transactions and sales		
Minimum number of sales transactions	N/A	100
Minimum amount of total sales	N/A	£1,000
Other criteria		
Member of the PowerSeller programme	–	Yes

What are the benefits of the discount scheme?

• Up to a 15% discount on final value fees.

• A badge on your listing pages.

• Improved visibility in 'Best Match' search results.

To say that things got a little complicated with the TRS scheme in the beginning is an understatement. Mollybol was a TRS for some months until 0.66% of my buyers decided my P&P charges were too high [Ed: you can't please everyone all the time]. A wholesale change to free P&P on all my listings now ensures a maximum score of 5 stars in this area and so this problem was solved. The TRS badge (these days shown as "eBay premium service") has been with me on three of my eBay trading IDs for some time now.

Defects

This section will attempt in a few words to explain the new measurement criteria for sellers – the defect rate. The basic idea here is that each time a buyer registers their displeasure about a trade then that seller will have a 'defect' recorded against their name. Too many defects and you lose your seller discounts. In extreme cases you could be removed from eBay altogether.

The actual criteria used by eBay to calculate this measurement are complex and there is not really much you can do about it – you just have to continue to offer the highest levels of service you can.

The defect rate is measured by these factors:

- Low detailed seller ratings for item as described (DSR score of 1, 2 or 3).
- Opened cases for items not as described.
- Returns for items not as described.
- Low detailed seller ratings for shipping time (DSR score of 1).
- Opened cases for items not received.
- Neutral or negative feedback from buyers.
- Cancelled transactions (out of stock or sold to someone else).

To retain Top-rated seller status your defect rate must remain below 2%. The good news, if there can be any, is that should a buyer open a case, leave you poor feedback and low DSR scores for the same transaction, then your defect rate will only take one hit.

One area where you may be able to reduce your defect rate is to steer your buyers away from opening a dispute case. In the past if a case was opened which you addressed then all was well, now just the action of opening a case will result in a defect against you. Previously, in an attempt to reduce buyer fraud for 'lost' items, I would insist that an 'Item not received' case was opened by the buyer, which would log the case against their name. After a time too many 'lost' items would lead someone to smell a rat. This is no longer possible because I would be bringing defects against myself and I now encourage buyers to email me directly.

If a buyer does open a case then I now add them to my 'Blocked bidder list' (BBL). Even if the problem is sorted I do not want to trade with them again just in case they follow the same route again in the future. This is probably not the outcome eBay would like to see and the individual buyer's future experience with me is not improved, but what else can I do?

You are able to monitor your defect performance via a report generated in your My eBay and what's more you can now see which transactions resulted in a low score. This is a positive move as often buyers will leave good feedback but mark you down on a DSR score. With a little detective work you can now discover who they were. Obviously these are also buyers that you would not wish to trade with again, so straight on to the BBL they go. My automatic emails now include a note saying that we welcome back buyers who leave 5 stars for the trade, inferring that any low score will result in that buyer being blocked.

This whole process is relatively new and eBay will amend it I am sure, as it is full of anomalies. For instance, there was the buyer who bought an item from me and then asked if it was genuine before I had dispatched it. Now this is a pet hate of mine and I do not want anything to do with a buyer who questions the authenticity of my items so I cancelled the trade, told them to shop at Debenhams and blocked them. Understandably they were a little miffed and left low DSR scores for 'Item as described' and 'Delivery time'. As the item was not sent – and never seen by them – how could they mark these scores low? This is just one example of how bonkers the whole thing is.

It is possible to contact eBay, explain your case and have inappropriate defects removed but this does take time and if you are around the 1% defect rate then it may not be worth the effort.

Things are always changing on eBay so we will all have to live with this process for the time being.

eBay motors

eBay has a separate fee structure for selling motor vehicles. Again you will pay an insertion fee and a final value fee (if the vehicle sells). An FVF scale is shown in Table 6. The main difference to other listings is the 'classified ad' option which is just the same as placing an ad in your local paper – eBay display the details for a fixed fee, with no bidding via the site. It's basically just an online advert.

Table 6. Final value fees for motor vehicles

		Classified	Auction	Buy It Now
Listing fees	Insertion fees	£14.99	£10.00	£10.00
Optional listing upgrades	Gallery Plus	£2.99	Free	Free
	Subtitle	£0.50	£0.50	£0.50
	Listing designer	Free	Free	Free
	Scheduler	Free	Free	Free
	Add Buy It Now	-	£2.99	-
	Reserve price	-	£7.99	-
Final value fees	Final value fee	-	1% final selling price (min. £20, max £35)	

Other fees

In addition to the eBay fees already covered, money deposited into your account via an electronic method may also incur a fee.

PayPal, for example, charges you for payments received. The fees are charged to your PayPal account and not your eBay account. More details on these charges will be given in the section concerning payment options.

Free listing days

On occasion, eBay will run promotions under which certain payment fees are altered or suspended for a day or maybe a whole weekend. These take several forms and can result in a considerable saving if you are able to exploit them when they occur. They tend to be for auctions listed by private sellers.

eBay do not give much notice when these promotions will run; you may only be notified by email on the preceding day.

The most common promotion used over recent months is a zero insertion fee for up to 100 listings.

 Take advantage of free listing days by listing a ten-day auction option which will incorporate the intermediate weekend.

Paying your fees

It is also worth mentioning at this time that as soon as you submit your item to eBay, the listing fee will be charged to your account, along with any listing upgrade fees. The final value fee will be calculated and charged when a sale is made.

You will receive a monthly invoice from eBay stating what fees you owe and eBay will automatically debit the amount via your selected payment method – either your bank account or credit card.

Summary

You should now:

- Know what eBay is.
- Know what equipment you need.
- Know when to sell and where to find stock.
- Have established your eBay account.
- Know who you are going to be selling to and where they are in the world.
- Understand eBay's fee structure.

You're now ready to start preparing for the first listing. On to the next chapter!

THREE

PREPARING FOR THE FIRST LISTING

Overview

The first eBay listing can be a little daunting. There are new skills to learn as you carry out the process for the first time. The key is to prepare before you begin so that when you are presented with a question during the process you will already have an idea of how you want to proceed. I will take you through what you need to consider in this chapter.

I will also tackle the research that is required to help you sell the right item at the right time. Using the eBay systems and search engines, it is possible to predict how successful your item will be in the current market and indicate how it may be possible to present it in a slightly different way to maximise the final sale price.

Before offering an item for sale, it is important to have an idea about what will happen when the listing ends. The size and weight of your package may well affect the delivery time to the buyer and considerations like this will alter the design of the listing. We will work through this process early in the chapter, because you will come to see that if you know how your item will be packed and sent before you begin, then creating the listing will become more straightforward.

You should also give some thought to listing design at this stage, so I cover this here, too.

Check the competition

It is now time to undertake specific research into the track record of the item you are intending to sell.

Using the search facility

You can use the eBay search facility to see how many items similar to the one you intend to sell are currently listed. By using the advanced search and ticking 'sold listings' you will get an indication of the prices that other listings of the item are fetching. If you select the 'completed listings' option then you will also see those items which didn't sell, perhaps because the price was too high or the time was not right for the sale. This can provide an invaluable insight as to the true value of your item.

If you are planning to sell an item that is not common on eBay then you may not be able to gather much information from the search, as there won't be many current or completed listings. If this is the case you may get an insight into value by using Google to find out retail prices. If, on the other hand, you are planning to sell a very common item then you may find that it has only been reaching a low price for other sellers, or there may be a lot of listings where the item has not sold at all.

Using the search facility before you start will save a lot of work if you learn that a particular item is not in demand and may not sell. It is always better to spend your time listing items for which there is demand as you are then more likely to get a sale and at a good price.

What are other sellers doing?

While you are checking out the competition to see how your item may perform, make some notes about the listings you visit. There is always a lot to be gained by seeing how other sellers present their items. Here are a few ideas:

- **Keywords in the title**. If other sellers are making sales of an item, they are very likely to be using the best key search words in their listings. Make a note of any terms that you think could be of use for your listings.

- **Starting price**. Check the starting prices of auctions; are they lower or higher than the price you were thinking of starting at?

- **Reserve price**. Are the other sellers using a reserve price? If so, is this affecting the bidding?

- **Format of listings**. Are the items offered in an auction format or are there any fixed-price listings?

- **Postage charges**. Compare the postage charges that sellers are applying. If they are much more than you were intending to charge, maybe the fact that you offer cheap postage could be placed into the title of your listing. A competitor's price may seem higher with postage added but if the second item has no additional postage charge then the total cost of two items may well be very attractive to a buyer.

- **Do other sellers post overseas?** Check to see if there is a relationship between the price an item has reached and the market that it is being sold into. The larger the market (i.e. if you sell worldwide), the higher the price should be. There are of course some items which weigh too much to make selling internationally economical, so consider this.

- **How many hits have the listings received?** If sellers have included a page views counter within their listings, check how many hits they have had. Does the use of keywords in the title have an impact on the number of visits? This might help with the selection of the search words that will drive the most customers to your listings.

 If you find that several sellers have a different postage charge to that which you were planning to charge, re-weigh your item and check the postage costs again, just to make sure you are correct.

Listing design

Now is the time to give some thought to how you want your listings to look. By working through some ideas before you start to sell there will be consistency in the appearance of your listings. Although the look will no doubt change over time, the basics will be in place.

Having an appealing design and layout is more likely to entice the visitor to do business with you. In a pleasant, well thought-out environment, buying will become more enjoyable. Imagine you are in a high street shop with very loud music, a gaudy colour scheme and a jumble of information at every turn. This may be the type of shop that appeals to you, or conversely it may in fact deter you from staying to browse the shop's products. An eBay listing is exactly the same. Design the layout and content appropriately for your target customers and they will buy from you, and return in the future to buy more.

It is possible to alter the appearance of almost anything within the eBay listing template, so you will see variations on the items you look at. Some will have borders around the edge, different colour backgrounds, moving text or pictures, multiple pictures and so on. As you browse existing listings on the site maybe you will discover a design that really appeals to you and gives you inspiration for your own design. The section below will touch on some of these areas that can be changed.

This is not intended to be a technical section, but a plan of how you want the finished design to look and feel. Some of the elements may require a little more technical knowledge and I will address this in later sections of the book.

Page format

Background colour

The standard background colour is white. You may be happy with this or wish to try something else.

Text colour

The default text colour is black. Depending on what you decide to do with the background colour, the text colour may need to be changed. One of the best attempts at 'keyword spamming' I have seen involved changing the colour of text to white on a white background. Visitors could not see the writing, but the eBay search engine found the words and displayed the item in results for searches of title and description.

Text size

The size of text is something that varies from seller to seller – you may have already noticed this. It is easy to alter text size, and larger text does have obvious advantages. However, if the item description is very detailed, larger text will make the page very long and difficult to read. It may be worth considering the use of titles within the description layout and adding weight to keywords and phrases.

Templates

A basic template has been constructed by eBay. It is essentially a blank space within which you can enter the description of your item. It is possible to use custom templates, which are available from the internet, and then copy them into your listing. These templates may have a cost associated with them, or some other requirements, such as credits to the author, which will need to be incorporated.

In a later section I will demonstrate how to create your own template using basic HTML code; this will allow you to fully customise your own look. If, however, you would prefer to use an existing template, check out some of the sites below:

• **Auction Insights** (www.auctioninsights.info/templates). Has a free online auction creator, just fill in the blanks and your eBay listing will appear.

- **Auction Supplies** (www.auctionsupplies.com/templates). Has the HTML code for a number of templates, just copy and paste it into the description of your listing.

If you are thinking of using an external template, check first that it will work on eBay.

When starting to sell on eBay, stick with the basic template and consider altering it as your experience grows.

Pictures

Having great pictures will certainly help encourage more sales. Even here, eBay gives you some options in terms of how many pictures you can include and how large you want them.

Picture size

eBay allows up to 12 pictures to be loaded into your listing for no charge. eBay recommends a picture with 1,600 pixels along the longest side, and there is a minimum size of 500 pixels on the longest side.

Multiple pictures

Some items are perfect for extra pictures: collectables, china, models, etc., will often be shown both from the back and front as the buyer will want to see the overall condition. Extra pictures will certainly help to sell these items.

I am very keen on extra pictures and would recommend that at least two are used. I will show you how to include extra pictures within your item description in a later section, but for now, think about whether your item could benefit from being shown with more than one picture.

Consider also items such as DVDs, CDs or computer games where there is a comprehensive description or track listing on the back of the case or box. To save time copying these out, just take a picture so that the buyer can read the detail directly from the packaging.

Close-up pictures may help to sell items as they suggest that the seller has nothing to hide. Use additional pictures to offer this view to customers.

When using close-up pictures, include a ruler or coin to give an idea of scale. If selling overseas, use a euro coin and maybe a dollar one, too, as these will be familiar to a wider market.

One of my favourite eBay stories (apparently completely true) relates to a seller of shoes receiving an email that said:

"You list the shoes as a size 6, but are they really a size 6, they look like a size 7? I wondered if there might be an error in the description."

Picture location

If you want to add pictures into your description then, the location is one of the most important elements of the whole design. Pictures at the top of the listing will catch the viewer's eye and convince them to read further about the item. Some simple HTML codes can be used to place pictures where you wish. If you are happy just to have the extra pictures that eBay host they will be shown in the main gallery picture area.

Links to additional pages

In your item description it is possible to include certain links to other websites. I will explain how this is achieved in a later section, but at this design stage consider the use of some of these links as they will provide your buyers with extra information. This will also reduce your workload as some frequently asked questions (FAQs) can be answered by following these links, meaning that buyers don't pepper you with questions by email.

eBay have very strict rules concerning the use of external links, but, as a general rule, if the destination site only offers information, it will be allowed.

I have listed below a few examples of links that you may consider. This is not an exhaustive list: remember that we want the buyer to stay focused on our product and not encourage them to wander too far into the wider internet. Send them to an information site by all means, but do not link to destinations that are more interesting than your own listing or they might forget about you as they surf off around the internet.

Currency converters

You might consider providing direct links to online currency converters – although there is also a currency converter within eBay (pages.eBay.co.uk/services/buyandsell/currencyconverter.html). Providing a link to a converter will reduce the number of questions you receive from overseas bidders regarding currency exchange rates. Some of the best currency converters I have found are:

- Bloomberg (www.bloomberg.com/invest/calculators/currency.html).

- Yahoo Finance (finance.yahoo.com/currency-converter).

- Oanda.com (www.oanda.com/currency/converter).

To use a converter, just type in the quantity that needs to be converted (e.g. 27.78), then select the type of currency that you have (e.g. UK pounds – often referred to as GBP) and then the currency that you want to convert into (e.g. US dollars).

Language translators

There are many free language translation websites. Although they may not translate perfectly, they are adequate to provide a good understanding of what is for sale. Two of the language converters I use most frequently are:

- BabelFish (www.babelfish.com).

- Free Translation (www.freetranslation.com).

To use the translator, just write in English the phrase you want to translate, select the appropriate 'to' and 'from' languages and click enter.

When using a translation service to construct a reply to an overseas enquiry, use simple phrases that are grammatically correct – this will increase the chances of a good translation.

Postal sites

A direct link to the Royal Mail website or another carrier site will demonstrate to your customers that your postage rates are not high (they can check if they wish). This may also save time as buyers can check any issues relating to insurance and delivery times themselves and they should email you less frequently. I have included a comprehensive list of postal services in a later section.

Links to your other listings

It's a great idea to show any potential buyers a selection of your other items that might appeal to them. There are a number of ways of achieving this:

- You could just mention in your description that you have other items for sale and hope that the visitor checks them out. If selling a pair of hiking boots, for example, you could write something along these lines: "If these boots are just what you are looking for, please check our other items where you will also find a great backpack and selection of walking sticks." To find these items, the potential customer would have to click on 'check our other items' to view your other listings and then click on the listing for, say, the walking sticks.

- The next option would be to have a similar statement about your items and also place a link directly to the page showing all of your listings next to it. This would remove one step. eBay have already created this link for you, it is just waiting to be used. eBay call this an *insert*. I will explain it fully later in the book.

- The third way would be to make part of your statement into a direct link to the actual listing. So in the phase we used above, the actual words 'backpack' and 'walking sticks' will become clickable links, taking your customer directly to the items. This option requires some knowledge of HTML, which is fully explained later in the book.

- The last method I will mention at this point is very similar to the above; still with a statement containing clickable links, but this time with a small picture of the actual item appearing alongside. This means your bidder can see the walking sticks, click on the picture and be taken directly to the item.

These cross-selling techniques will drive your sales and can be used to increase the number of visits to an item that is not performing very well.

Links to pages containing additional content and pictures

It may be useful to have links within your listings that refer the visitor to another web page for additional pictures and your terms and conditions. This will help with the load time of your main listing page and remove some of the clutter.

Linking to these extra web pages is a little more advanced and is covered in the later section concerning the development of your eBay activity.

 Only include supplementary information – and not essential information – on additional pages as not everybody will click through to them and you don't want visitors missing your key messages.

The eBay linking policy – what is and is not allowed

eBay have very strict rules about what kind of links can be placed within an item description. For a full breakdown, visit the eBay help pages: pages.ebay.co.uk/help/policies/listing-links.html

In summary, these are the links that are currently allowed:

Links allowed

- One link to a page that further describes the item being sold in that listing.
- One link to your email address for potential buyers to ask questions about the item in that listing.
- Links to photos of the item for sale.
- Links to your other eBay listings (including your eBay shop).
- Links that provide credits to third parties such as picture hosts or template designers.
- One link to your listing terms and conditions.

 Why not consider translating your terms and conditions into other languages and including additional links to them from your listings?

Links not allowed

Certain links are not allowed. The list below is not comprehensive, but does indicate the kinds of links you can't use:

- Links to web pages that offer to trade, sell or purchase goods or services outside of eBay. This applies whether it is a static URL or an active link. Naturally eBay want the trade to be completed on the site so they can collect their fees.

- Links to websites or pages offering merchandise.

- Links to sites that solicit eBay User IDs or passwords from buyers.

- Links that encourage buyers to place their eBay bids through a site other than eBay. When I discuss *affiliate sales* later in this book, you will see that it is possible to earn money by sending customers to eBay. You are not allowed to direct a buyer out of eBay on to an affiliate site and then back again, making a few pounds along the way.

- Links or other connections to live chat systems.

 If in any doubt about whether you can use a particular link, email the eBay support team and ask them.

External web space

If you have some internet web space already, it is possible to use that to host additional pages for your listings. You may have some web space available through your internet service provider (ISP), or you may have chosen to purchase it from another supplier. Either way, this additional space is a great way to present information to your customers without having too much detail cluttering up your item listings.

If you don't already have web space of your own, but would like to look into it further, check out these sites:

- 50 Megs (www.50megs.com). This site offers a range of services including free hosting space to get you started. To get enough space, you will need to pay for the service. A good package is Starter Hosting, which costs $3.95 per month (about £2.50, depending on the current exchange rate). The package includes:

  - 1000 MB web space.

  - 10 GB of bandwidth per month.

  - 50 MB file size limit

I currently use 50 MB to host my pictures along with a number of other web pages that I have built. This service costs me about £4 per month for 5000 MB of storage space.

- Bravenet (www.bravenet.com). This provider also offers a free package and several other options based on the length of your contract. The one-year package costs $8.25 per month (about £5) and it includes the following:
  - 600 GB of monthly bandwidth.

  - 30 GB disk space.

  - Unlimited pop3 email accounts.

  - Free domain name.

  - Unlimited sub domains.

  - Unlimited FTP accounts.

Check that the option you choose will allow pictures stored on it to be viewed on eBay; the free services may not allow this.

Personal or business-like?

The decision to make your listings formal or informal will depend very much upon your own style and the items you are going to sell. There is no hard and fast rule. As you look through other eBay auctions and shop listings, you will see examples of both styles. Use the method you feel most comfortable with.

Right from the very beginning I decided to make my listings as informal as possible. There are no strict deadlines about payment or who is allowed to bid or buy; I believe that this approach works well for my type of business.

Your trading terms and conditions

Setting out how you will do business in the form of your terms and conditions (Ts&Cs) seems such an obvious thing to do, as it will make transactions easier if buyers know what to expect. However, it's surprising just how many eBay sellers do not present this information. Deciding how you will trade before you start should ensure that every one of your transactions has a good chance of a successful conclusion.

As a seller, you will have considerable control over your eBay listings and can impose almost any conditions you see fit. The following are just some of the areas where you will have control:

- Which areas of the world you will do business with.
- Who pays for postage costs, including any insurance premiums.
- Which postal services you will offer.
- How long it will be before you post the item.
- How long you will give buyers to pay for items they have won.
- Which payment methods you will accept.
- Whether you will sell to buyers with less than, say, ten feedbacks.
- You can block any eBay user you don't want to trade with.

You can decide how you will trade and the buyer must fall in line with you or you can refuse to complete the trade. I would just make a note of caution at this point: the harder your trading terms are, the fewer buyers you are likely to attract. It is a balancing act.

Distance selling regulations

Buying anything over the internet or by phone can be tricky as you cannot hold the item and check it thoroughly. To help buyers in the UK, legislation was passed in 2000 giving buyers certain rights when they buy online (or by mail order). These rights apply to fixed-price sales made on eBay by business-registered sellers. Even if this does not apply to you and your items, it is good practice to observe these rules anyway.

This is what eBay has to say on the subject:

Under the Consumer Protection (Distance Selling) Regulations 2000 you have to refund an item if the buyer changes their mind within 7 working days after the day on which the item was delivered.

The Distance Selling Regulations generally apply to sales to non-business buyers made by sellers acting in the course of a business, which have been made at a distance. In other words, where there is no face-to-face contact between the seller and the buyer before the contract is made. The Distance Selling Regulations usually cover sales made over the internet, including:

— Buy It Now listings on eBay.co.uk

— Second Chance Offers on eBay.co.uk

The UK Distance Selling Regulations do not apply to auction-style format listings on eBay.co.uk, and do not apply to all types of items.

If your listing doesn't fall under the Distance Selling Regulations, you're not legally obliged to refund a buyer if they change their mind. However, you may choose to provide a service that goes beyond the minimum legal requirement in order to encourage consumers to buy from you.

Under the Distance Selling Regulations, buyers have a period of 7 working days after the date of delivery within which they can cancel the contract (often referred to as the "cooling off" period) and get their money back, including the original postage and packing charges. You must refund the original delivery charges. You are permitted to require the buyer to pay for the cost of returning the item, but only if you clearly inform the buyer of this before the contract is made.

You can specify the returns time frame and who pays for return postage when you create your returns policy. Please note that the minimum time frame for returns on eBay is 14 days.

There is more information on the eBay help pages: pages.ebay.co.uk/businesscentre/returnsandthelaw.html

How and where to display your Ts&Cs

How you tell visitors about your terms and conditions of trading will depend upon the final design of your listing template. You may wish to have them attached to each listing, or on a separate internet page via an interactive link.

After much consideration I decided to keep my actual listings as short as possible and have my trading terms on a separate page. I feel that it keeps my page load time low and does not distract my buyers from the item for sale. I allow a 14-day return period in line with the eBay requirements for Top-rated sellers but ask that return postage is paid by the buyer. More on the infamous Top-rated seller (TRS) scheme later.

Create a pleasant environment

When writing your Ts&Cs, try not to be too aggressive – make your point, but word it in such a way that a visitor will not feel intimidated. If you require payment within seven days, explain why (maybe you have had several non-payers).

If you will not accept bids from new members, ask them to email you for help and assistance rather than stating that they cannot bid. Remember, people buy from people they can relate to and people they like. If you are struggling for the right words, check out a few stores when next shopping on the high street; these guys spend thousands getting their policies just right.

What to include in your Ts&Cs

Exactly what you decide to include within your Ts&Cs will depend on the kind of customers you want to sell to and where in the world they are. It is quite likely that you will change these conditions over time as you gain an insight into the kind of problems that can occur.

There are a few standard terms that you may wish to consider from the beginning:

- Postage terms.
- Returns policy.
- Payments policy.

Let's look at these three key areas in more detail.

1. Postage terms

Setting out your postage terms before you list your items will ensure that your customers will know what to expect. Once an item has been bought or won, the buyer or winning bidder will want their item as soon as possible but you can manage their expectations by stating what will happen in the item listing.

Dispatch and delivery times

eBay requires that all listings include a dispatch time. I aim to post items on the same day on which payment is made, so I opt for a one-day dispatch time just in case I have too many coffee breaks and run out of time.

Some sellers will only post on certain days of the week. This will cut down on trips to the Post Office, but will lead to delays in delivery. If you intend to clear funds before you dispatch the item, include these timescales so that your buyer can anticipate when to expect the item.

How you intend to send the item will also impact on the delivery time; again, put the postal services you offer into your postage terms. If you intend to partake in the TRS programme then you will need to offer free postage as your first domestic postage option and also an express next-day delivery service. Start to give some thought to this now and I'll run through the pros and cons in due course.

Consider the situation where a buyer buys several small items from you in one go, pushing the now larger package into parcel post bandings, which in turn may take longer to deliver.

Postal services

As you will see when I look at the topic of placing your first listing, you will be able to offer four domestic UK postal services for an item and state the appropriate costs. There is a drop-down menu of options – just select the one you need for each postal service. International postage details can be selected in much the same way with different options given for specific locations.

Current postage options are summarised in Table 7.

Table 7. Postage options

UK postal options	International postal options
Royal Mail 1st Class and 2nd Class	Royal Mail International Standard
Royal Mail Signed For	Royal Mail International Tracked
Royal Mail Special Delivery, 9am or 1pm	Royal Mail International Signed
Parcelforce Worldwide	Royal Mail International Tracked & Signed
Other courier or delivery service	Royal Mail International Economy (Surface Mail)
	Parcelforce Worldwide
	Other courier or delivery service

eBay estimates the delivery time of your item based on the postage service you offer and the number of days within which you dispatch. This is only an estimate but does influence buyers and can cause problems when an item is delayed, as expectations have been set.

From the choice of postal services that you offer for your item, your buyer can choose the method that suits them best. The more options you can offer, the more likely you are to make a sale.

The two main extra choices I offer in addition to the required ones are 'Royal Mail International Signed' and 'Royal Mail International Standard (Small Packets)'. These international options are only offered for my Toy and DIY businesses. I no longer send cosmetics overseas as the contents could contain flammable ingredients (perfume & nail varnish), or they could be mistaken for flammable at customs and destroyed.

 eBay now requires all listings to include at least one domestic postal service and P&P cost associated with this, so buyers will know exactly what the total costs are before they buy. This should reduce the number of questions you receive about this and therefore save you time.

Proof of postage

The Royal Mail will cover most items for a minimum amount should they become lost or damaged whilst in their system. However, this is not always the case and should not be relied on. There is a standard proof of postage form which can be completed and stamped by the Post Office at the time of dispatch.

Always obtain a proof of postage (PoP). It's free and will provide you with a chance of recovering some money should an item not arrive. I will talk about this compensation policy again later as it is fair to say that I am not a big fan and personally I don't bother claiming for lost parcels as the Royal Mail has never coughed up yet. However, for now, just concentrate on the fact of stating that you will obtain PoP in your Ts&Cs. At least your customers will be aware of this.

Liability statement

It is quite common for eBay sellers to state that the posting of an item does not guarantee delivery and that the liability for chasing a lost parcel lies with the buyer. Unless you have proof of delivery then in my experience eBay (and their payment arm PayPal) will always side with the buyer in the case of a lost item dispute. Business sellers are responsible for the parcel until it is safely delivered, so if it gets lost (stolen) or damaged in transit – ouch, it hurts!

Multiple purchases

Will you offer a reduction in postage costs for multiple purchases? This may save you packing time and may also encourage customers to buy more items.

2. Returns policy

Having a returns policy will provide your buyer with the confidence that should anything not be as expected, they can return the item. This should increase your sales, but give some serious thought to the wording you use so that returning an item is the last resort for a buyer. Here are just a few things to consider when setting out your returns policy:

- Will you provide full money back or a credit note?
- Will you refund the return postage as well as the item cost?
- How long will you allow for a buyer to return an item?
- What grounds will you accept for a refund?

Don't make your returns policy too easy or you may find that you are always dealing with returns. You are in this to make money, not to offer a try before you buy service!

Business sellers are obliged to offer a returns policy of at least 14 days but it could be as long as 60 days. Most Buy It Now purchases are covered under the Distance Selling Regulations discussed above, which give consumers the right to cancel the purchase within seven working days after the day they receive the item. You are legally obliged to inform consumers about their right of cancellation before the purchase.

3. Payments policy

When deciding upon a payments policy, you may consider having one set of options for UK customers and another for international buyers, based upon the costs of each service. I will discuss the alternatives for receiving payment in more detail in the next section, along with some costs.

How long will you allow before payment should be received?

Just how long you will wait before chasing for payment is an important decision. It may depend on the value of the item, how much stock you have, or the feedback history of the buyer. Each case may be different. However, having a general rule will let the buyer know what is expected of them.

Payment clearance times

For a payment option that takes some time to clear, such as a personal cheque, state how long it will be before you send the item. Cheques clear in about five working days, so just put this into your trading terms. Electronic cheques (eCheques) also take some time to clear (although they can arrive via the PayPal system) and should be treated as traditional cheques.

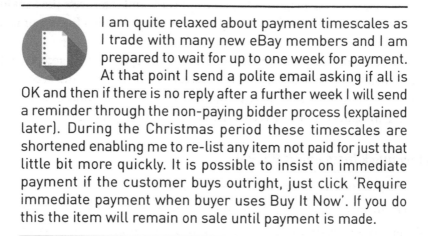

I am quite relaxed about payment timescales as I trade with many new eBay members and I am prepared to wait for up to one week for payment. At that point I send a polite email asking if all is OK and then if there is no reply after a further week I will send a reminder through the non-paying bidder process (explained later). During the Christmas period these timescales are shortened enabling me to re-list any item not paid for just that little bit more quickly. It is possible to insist on immediate payment if the customer buys outright, just click 'Require immediate payment when buyer uses Buy It Now'. If you do this the item will remain on sale until payment is made.

Payment options

Let's be honest, you will be paid via PayPal. It's a no brainer for buyers, free to use, easy and if anything goes wrong PayPal will side with them every time. Sure there are other options, I still receive a few cheques each year and some buyers, particularly in Germany, love to use bank transfer. You can decide which payment methods you will accept, I'll briefly mention some others below but prepare yourself for PayPal and all its associated costs.

The payment options are:

1. PayPal.

2. Cash payment on collection.

3. Credit cards.

4. Bank deposit.

5. Personal cheque.

6. Postal order.

1. PayPal

It is compulsory for all sellers to accept PayPal, with the exception of listings in the categories of cars, motorcycles, aircraft, boats, caravans, trailers, trucks (commercials), services and property. eBay owns PayPal, so you can see why they would want to enforce this.

PayPal enables consumers to send and receive money via their computers. PayPal is a truly global company with millions of users throughout the world.

It can handle all of the major credit and debit cards and can access the banking infrastructure to enable funds to be deposited to and withdrawn from your bank account.

It is a quick and easy way for businesses and entrepreneurs to accept credit card payments online without having to establish a merchant bank account to do so. PayPal enables any business or consumer with an email address to securely, conveniently and cost-effectively send and receive these payments.

A few quick facts about PayPal

- PayPal does not have a set-up charge for either buyers or sellers.
- There are mechanisms in place to protect the buyer and seller from fraud.
- Payments are made to your email address, which acts as an account ID number.
- The fee structure is easy to understand, but the fees can be high – up to 3.4% of the value of money transacted.
- Sending money directly to another PayPal account is easy and the transfer is very quick.
- Withdrawals can be made into your bank account once your account has been 'verified'. It can take up to five days for the money to transfer to your bank but in my experience it is often instant.
- Partial refunds can be made through the system, which will mean that if you refund some postage, for example, you will also recover some of the fees you paid on the original transaction, but not the fixed cost associated with each transaction – which is commonly 20p.
- PayPal has a range of merchant tools which may help your administration processes. The history function is very useful when calculating turnover, for example.

For the buyer, PayPal is very easy to use, the payment is instant and therefore their item can be sent quickly.

PayPal operates a two-tier charging structure. For every payment that is made the seller will pay a flat charge and then a percentage on the total monetary value, which includes the P&P. For most PayPal accounts in the UK the flat fee is 20p and the percentage charged is 3.4%. Merchants (sellers with a higher volume of PayPal transaction value) pay a lower percentage rate (see Tables 8 and 9).

PayPal fees

The fees for PayPal transactions are based on total value received into your account in the previous month. They are shown in Tables 8 and 9.

Table 8. Receipts from UK customers

Receipts	Fees
£0.00 – £1,500	3.4% + £0.20
£1,500.01 – £6,000	2.9% + £0.20
£6,000.01 – £15,000	2.4% + £0.20
£15,000.01 – £55,000	1.9% + £0.20
above £55,000	1.4% + £0.20

Table 9. Receipts from customers outside the UK

Receipts	Fees
£0.00 – £1,500	3.9% + £0.20
£1,500.01 – £6,000	3.4% + £0.20
£6,000.01 – £15,000	2.9% + £0.20
£15,000.01 – £55,000	2.4% + £0.20
above £55,000	1.9% + £0.20

To check your fee structure log in to your PayPal account in the normal way and type fees into the search box at the top of the page. Then click on a link to the fees page. Your fees rate will be shown. You can access your cross-border rate from this location as well.

Do not underestimate the impact of the 20p transaction fee, they soon add up. As a merchant seller my monthly percentage fees are usually 1.9%. As my average sale price is around £10 this means that I pay more in 20p flat fees than I do as a percentage of my throughput. With a turnover of £200,000 per year I end up paying around £4,000 just in the 20p flat fee.

Send money to friends and family for free with PayPal

- Log in.
- Click 'Send Money'.
- Enter email address, amount and currency.
- Select 'I'm sending money to family or friends'.
- Click continue to complete the transaction.

No fees are applied to this transaction.

Require immediate payment?

You have the option to 'Require immediate payment' from your buyer – if you activate this, then until the buyer actually pays, the item will remain on sale. eBay is likely to implement this policy for all purchases using all payment options in the future, which is not going to be welcome at Molly HQ. The thought of having to pay even more 20p transaction fees is not very attractive.

Micro-payments

If you sell items with a combined end price including P&P of £9.50 or below then it may be cost effective for you to open a PayPal micro-payments account. This account is exactly the same as the standard one, but has a different charging setup. The fixed fee drops to 5p and the percentage increases to 5%. This means that for values of £9.50 or lower the micro-payments account will save you money.

For example, for a sale of £3.00 (sale price and postage) the micro-payments account fees are 20p (5% of £3 plus 5p for the transaction).

With a traditional premier account (macro) the fees are 30p (3.4% of £3 plus 20p for the transaction).

The micro-payments account will save you 10p on this transaction.

If you generally use the micro-payments account but on a specific occasion sell multiple low-value items to a single customer and this comes in at more than £9.50, alter the PayPal details to your main account (the non-micro payments account) when you send a combined invoice to the buyer. This will reduce your fees.

You can change your main PayPal account to the micro-payments system or if you prefer you can open a new account and direct all of your smaller payments into it. I have two PayPal accounts and use the micro-payments account for cheaper Buy It Now (BIN) items – the savings soon add up.

To activate a micro-payments account it looks as if you need to contact PayPal directly (which is a change from the situation in the past). Put the kettle on before you call them.

When it comes to receiving money, I accept only PayPal for my cosmetics business. This is due to my agreed VAT payment structure whereby I send 8% of all monies received through my PayPal account to HMRC, I'll explain more about this in the VAT section later. The easier you make it for buyers to pay, the more likely you are to make more sales and more profit. Some buyers would prefer not to pay electronically, so consider a range of other payment methods.

2. Cash payment on collection

Cash is no longer permitted as a payment option on eBay as it is not traceable and there is no way to prove that the payment was received.

Cash on collection, however, is still possible because if you choose to you can allow a buyer to pay you in cash when they arrive to pick up your second-hand bed, or whatever the item is. However, you cannot advertise this in your listing.

Instead you must include a phrase along the lines of "contact us for payment details." Adding the word "cash" into the listing is not allowed. It seems a crazy rule, but it's not worth falling out with eBay over this.

3. Credit cards

To accept credit card payments you will need the appropriate banking systems in place. For individuals this is not easy and can be costly. The majority of small sellers on eBay do not accept credit cards and a close substitute is of course PayPal.

4. Bank deposit

The ability for the buyer to deposit money directly into a branch of your bank is great for sellers, as it is deposited as cash and is therefore available straightaway. Transfers between different UK banks can take up to four days although quite often they are instant these days.

Accepting money from another account in the UK is, as far as I am aware, free of any transaction costs. This is not necessarily the case when accepting money transfers from overseas.

To receive international payments you will need to obtain some details from your bank: these are known as IBAN and BIC or Swift codes. You will need to give these along with the name of your bank to your buyer, who will then make the transfer.

I do not receive many requests to accept international money transfers. If I do get such a request I always ask the buyer to pay any associated fees.

5. Personal cheques

Personal cheques are still a common means of payment, especially by buyers who do not want, or cannot get, an online account of any kind. Receiving a cheque is great as it can be deposited without any charges, unless you use a business account or deposit too many cheques. As your business grows, you may need to deposit cheques into a separate business account.

You can also accept personal cheques from overseas buyers that are drawn in other currencies. Depending on who you bank with, you may find that cheques up to a value of £30 can usually be exchanged for no charge; the banks negotiate them with each other (e.g. Halifax currently offers this service). Offering to take personal cheques in other currencies may increase your international business.

 If your item sells for more than £30, just ask the international buyer to send more than one cheque and then present them to your bank one at a time.

The exchange rate that you receive from your bank may not be that favourable and the money does take a while to be credited to your account. You will need to decide if this is worth offering as an additional payment option.

 When sending your invoice to a successful buyer, include a short note detailing who the cheque should be made payable to. I have received cheques made out to Molly Bol, which proves very difficult to clear through the bank.

6. Postal orders

The traditional postal order is great for sellers as there are no fees for cashing them in; simply take them to your local Post Office and hand them over. If they are crossed, simply pay them into your bank as you would a standard cheque. The buyer will have to pay a fee when the postal order is purchased and this can be quite high depending on the value.

The major drawback with postal orders comes as you may encounter delays at the Post Office when trying to cash them and time spent queuing is lost money. Ask your buyer to send a crossed postal order and then pay it directly into your bank.

 If you think that a buyer may be paying with a postal order and the item has a low price, offer them the alternative of sending ordinary postage stamps instead. They will save the postal order fees, you will not have to queue to cash the order and postage stamps are always useful for eBay sellers!

Make receiving money easy

- Embrace PayPal and smile! It does cost money, but PayPal is now understood by most bidders and you have no choice but to offer this option anyway.

- Bank deposits might be an option if your target market has a preference. Obtain the information from your bank that will allow bank transfers from overseas. Ensure that the buyer pays any fees.

- Check with your bank and see if they will clear foreign personal cheques without making a charge. There is bound to be an upper limit, so include this in your trading terms.

- Clear funds before dispatch. It sounds like common sense, but ensuring the funds have cleared before you send the item will save a lot of time sorting out problems. Remember that eCheques need time to clear.

Prepare your item

Before you list an item a little preparation will help the item sell and reach the best possible price. It may seem like an obvious thing to do, but if you have already looked at a range of listings on eBay then you will know that many sellers do not prepare their items for sale properly.

So, here are some recommendations when preparing your item to sell:

- **Clean it**. Take the time to ensure your item looks its best. If it has been stored, brush off the dust and remove any marks that can be seen. Close-up pictures will show every aspect of the item, including any blemishes, so remove these if you can.

- **Mend it**. Repair items that are damaged or which need replacement parts if you can. For example, just changing the hub caps on a car will improve the overall look and the first impression.

- **Present it**. Stage your pictures and be creative. Try to suggest how the item could be used. If selling furniture for a doll's house, prepare a room setting rather than just laying out the items for the picture. Take close-up pictures of any key pieces. If you sell clothes, fold them neatly and arrange them in the picture, use hangers if they help or even invest in a tailor's dummy. As all pictures are now free, take loads and choose the best ones later.

Packaging materials

The packaging of your item is one of the things that you will be judged on as a seller – how the item arrives at the buyer's address will determine the kind of feedback you receive. Broken, scratched or otherwise damaged items will not make the buyer feel as though they have traded with somebody who really cares. They may not visit you again and may also mention the packing quality in their feedback.

Send items in such a way that you would be pleased to see them arrive at your own door. Even if the item sold for only a small amount, send it on its way with care as the buyer may return for a larger purchase later.

The huge variety of goods that can be sold on eBay means it's difficult to be specific here about what is best for packing individual items, but there are some general points to bear in mind and I will discuss these.

What you will need

There is a vast range of packaging materials available. These can of course be purchased from a variety of stores, including from eBay itself.

However, running a successful eBay business involves keeping costs as low as possible so when you are starting to sell you should recycle anything that you can for use as packing materials. You can also visit local stores such as supermarkets to see if they are disposing of anything that could be of use.

Bubble wrap

The best invention ever made for an eBay seller! It is light, strong and not too expensive. The size of the bubbles does vary, so if you are going to order without seeing the actual wrap, make sure you get the correct size for your items.

Order your bubble wrap through eBay. As you can see in the screenshot below, there's plenty of competition in this market and you will often get a good deal.

Fig 7. Search for bubble wrap

Boxes

Boxes can of course be purchased through eBay and in a variety of shapes and sizes. They will be sent flat, so you will have to assemble them before items can be packed.

Don't get too hung up on a specific size of box as the less popular sizes may cost more. A four-inch square box may cost more than a five-inch square one as it is less popular, so sending items in the larger box may prove better value for you. Remember though that if you go for a large box size you may need to include extra packing materials to protect smaller items, so it is a balancing act.

One thing to aim for is a box that when assembled is less than 150mm square as this is the maximum size of box that is treated as a 'small parcel' by the Royal Mail's policy and the saving on postage you'll make here is considerable.

Below is an example of what you are likely to pay for 25 boxes of various sizes on eBay:

- Size 127 x 127 x 127mm – £7.90.

- Size 203 x 152 x 102mm – £10.70.

- Size 305 x 229 x 127mm – £14.90.

- Size 279 x 254 x 115mm – £16.30.

- Size 432 x 254 x 153mm – £19.80.

 Cut off some of the flaps or other superfluous bits from boxes to save on weight and therefore cost when posting. The box must remain strong enough, however!

Bubble bags

Bubble bags also come in an assortment of sizes and – surprise, surprise – the bigger they are, the more they cost. Also, buying just one bag at a time as you sell an item will work out very expensive. Check local wholesalers in your area and buy in quantities of at least 100 to get the price of each bag down to a reasonable level. You should use the smallest bags you can for your items to make an extra saving on costs.

Table 10 provides examples of what you are likely to pay for 100 of each of the most popular bag sizes on eBay, along with an idea of what will fit in them. Be a little cautious if you opt for the smallest bag as they have a habit of disappearing more easily in the postal system.

Table 10. Example bubble bag costs

Bag size	Cost for 100 units	Suggested item
Size A (110 x 160mm)	£4.70	jewellery, watches
Size B (120 x 210mm)	£6	small items
Size C (150 x 210mm)	£6	CDs
Size D (180 x 260mm, A5)	£7.50	DVD/VHS tapes
Size E (220 x 260mm)	£10	small giftware
Size F (220 x 330mm)	£14	small books, software
Size G (240 x 330mm, A4)	£14	brochures, literature
Size H (270 x 360mm)	£20	larger books
Size J (300 x 440mm)	£26	small clothing
Size K (350 x 470mm, A3)	£29	

Check out some of the high street discount shops – such as The Range and Poundland – as they often have reasonably priced bubble bags if you just need a few. For larger quantities use eBay.

Parcel wrapping paper

To add extra security or a professional touch to your parcels, consider wrapping them in brown paper. This can be purchased on large rolls, but these may well work out to be too heavy to buy on the internet because the delivery charges will be very high. Instead, check for suppliers in your area and buy several rolls in one visit.

Tape

Sticky tape will be used on almost every item: parcel tape for the actual package, clear tape to hold things together while you pack them and maybe also 'Fragile' tape if your item is breakable.

Where to source the materials

• **When starting out.** Don't throw anything away: recycle boxes and bubble bags from any items you buy, and obtain bubble wrap from the grocery department at your local supermarket. I still even now collect unwanted boxes from the guy who sells biscuits and cakes at my local car boot sale. I flat-pack them and take them all home; it probably is not worth the time and effort any more but I just can't help myself.

- **Retail outlets**. Check your local high street discount stores. Reduce costs where possible but still try to buy something that will do the job. Cheaper tape will save you money, but keep some better quality tape for parcels to be sent overseas by surface mail, as it will need to hold together for up to eight weeks.

- **eBay sellers**. There are many sellers of packing materials on eBay. There will be a delivery overhead here but with a little planning you will be able to order in bulk. (And, of course, you will collect another feedback rating for the transaction.)

 Invest in an electric paper shredder (you can buy one from Argos for about £25). Shredded paper makes great packing material and you will finally have a use for all the unsolicited mail that comes through your letterbox.

Storage

Storing your packing materials can be a problem and you should give some thought to this before you order a large quantity. It could be a safety hazard as these materials are combustible and you also need to have them to hand when you are packing to save as much time as possible.

This is the one area I completely underestimated when designing my office (shed). Just after a large order there are bubble bags everywhere, cardboard boxes on shelves that should contain stock and the family has to sit on bubble wrap when watching TV.

That special touch

How your buyer receives their item may well determine if they will visit you again. They will expect what they purchased to be delivered in a timely manner, but will also expect the packaging to be of a certain standard. Getting this final aspect correct will make all the difference.

Take that little bit of extra care when packing and turn this into one of your key selling points: "Trade with us and we promise top quality packaging." This may just place you one step ahead of the competition and it need not cost you much more to achieve.

Include a note of thanks

It is always a nice touch to include a note with the item thanking the buyer for their business. You can easily print this out at home yourself.

Why not take it a little further and ask the bidder to visit again for more great items? Reassure them that should anything not be as they had expected with the item, you will put things right. Occasionally things do go wrong and it is much better for the buyer to contact you first rather than leave negative feedback, so include this on your note.

Addressing

Ensure the package is addressed correctly

On the front of the package, write clearly, or print the delivery address, using all of the address including the postcode. This way you give the parcel the best chance of arriving at the correct address.

When sending heavy items, write the weight on the front; the Post Office workers will thank you for this.

Include a return address label

Adding a return address is a good idea. Not many items get lost, but if they do, there is always the chance the package can be sent back to you. The most common cause is when a parcel is not collected by the recipient from their local depot and in this case the return label should ensure it finds its way back to you.

As an aside on this subject, if a parcel is returned to you for this reason don't resend it, just cancel the transaction and refund the buyer. Then ensure you block the buyer (details of how to do this are included later in the book) because if they didn't collect the package once they may well not do so again, and it is a waste of your time and money to keep sending it to them.

Writing out the return address on each parcel can become a bit tedious, so consider having some labels printed. You can usually get these done for a reasonable price. Include the word 'From' or 'Sender' at the top, and at the end of the address add 'UK'. Then when sending overseas you won't have to keep adding these extra words. I get all my return labels from eBay (stores.ebay.co.uk/SkarlettNoire). 2,000 labels of size 38.1mm by 21.2mm will set you back £3.85 delivered.

Five tips for top-class packaging

1. **Over-protect your items**. Damaged items cause bad feeling, they can cost time and money to put right and could result in bad feedback. Pack everything well first time.

2. **Establish a stock of packing materials**. You cannot afford to run out of packing materials. Make sure there are enough boxes or bags available.

3. **Recycle anything that can be re-used**. Particularly in the early days, re-use anything that you can. It will save money and it is good for the environment.

4. **Decide how to pack the item before you sell it**. Plan ahead with your packaging and you will be able to pack and send the item much quicker when the auction ends. You will also be able to get a better postage estimate, which will help you price more accurately.

5. **Packing area and time**. Having a dedicated area for packing is a good idea; it saves time if you don't have to get all the materials out and then put them away again each time. If this is not possible, do your packing in one session, once per day. It will save time.

One of my lost parcels returned from the Netherlands after seven weeks and I have had a fancy dress costume returned from the Czech Republic, so return labels have worked for me.

Posting your item

This section concerns postage – both the charges and the companies that offer delivery services. I will deal mainly with the services from the Royal Mail as these are likely to be the most commonly used, but I also discuss some of the other carriers.

Postage charges are a major element of costs and, obviously, the higher the postage charge you levy to customers, the higher the overall cost of your items. In my experience most buyers will consider the total cost of an item – including the price of the item itself and delivery – when shopping on eBay. So if your postage charges are high this may well restrict the price that your item will sell for. Buyers like to know postage charges upfront, as this will allow them to appreciate the full cost of the item before they buy.

Carriers

Royal Mail

For most items, you are likely to use the Post Office, so visit their website at www.royalmail.com and bookmark the page showing the postage rates for both first and second class mail within the UK, and the overseas airmail and surface mail rates, or print the pricing tables off and keep them somewhere safe. You then have these to hand for your reference.

For 2014 you can find these rates here, but bear in mind the last part of this address will change with the year: www.royalmail.com/prices-2014

Domestic service

The current UK domestic pricing structure includes options for sending items classed as either letter, large letter, small parcel (including wide and deep options) and medium parcel.

Get to know these services as you may be able to package your item in a slightly different way and cut down on postage costs. What deal you can get will impact on your decision on whether to use the Royal Mail or not and this will in turn have an impact on delivery times, which your buyer should be informed of upfront.

Letters are fairly straightforward – these are items that are no more then 5mm thick and typical letter-sized in terms of width and height (240mm x 165mm). Large letters are not too bad to get to grips with either – these are to be no more than 25mm (one inch in old money) thick and about the dimensions of an A4 piece of paper.

It is the parcel pricing which gets a bit convoluted; apart from the length and width it is the thickness which determines if the parcel is small or medium. Anything over 80mm thick becomes a medium parcel, regardless of weight, so a soft cuddly teddy is a medium parcel whereas a heavy central heating valve travels as a small parcel. There are a couple of exceptions but generally speaking if your item falls into the medium parcel bracket with Royal Mail then look for another carrier.

 Search eBay for 'new 2nd class stamps' and save around 13%.

International services

International postage services are also available from the Royal Mail and there are a number to choose from. Table 11 shows the range of services and gives an indication of their cost at the time of writing.

For full information visit the Royal Mail website, where you can download a PDF of the full range of prices for various services and weights of parcel: www.royalmail.com/prices-2014

Table 11. Royal Mail international services

Service	Benefits
International Tracked & Signed	Tracked for full journey and a signature is taken at the point of delivery. This service is available to 43 countries and starts at £8.20 for a very light parcel of 100g or less. The rates increase by weight from 100g upwards.
International Tracked	Fast, secure and reliable airmail with electronic tracking to 33 destinations. Parcels will receive priority handling in the UK and abroad. Starts at £9.84 for a very light parcel of 100g.
International Signed	Tracked for the UK part of the journey and a signature is taken at the point of delivery. This service is available to almost every country (190 in fact) and starts at £8.20 for a very light parcel of 100g or less. The rates increase by weight from 100g upwards.
International Standard	Parcels can be sent virtually anywhere in the world with prices starting at £3.20 for a 100g parcel. Most mail is delivered within three to five days, depending on destination.

Use a set of digital scales when weighing your items. Mistakes can be very expensive so you want to be as accurate as possible. Royal Mail airmail rates rise in tiers, so it is easy to lose profit by guessing what the postage costs will be only to find that when packed it has crept into the next price band.

Online Business Account (OBA)

You can register for a business account with the Royal Mail. This allows you to sort your own mail, bag and tag it, and drop it at your local depot, with no need to queue at the Post Office. I have done this for my cosmetic business.

The easiest way to find out if the OBA will work for you is to give the Royal Mail a call on 08457 950 950.

Using the OBA is easy – you just select a code that reflects the service you want to use, enter the number of items and their average weight on the website and the system calculates the price for you.

For me the standard services work out as the best options and so most often I use just three codes:

1. BPL – standard letters, large for all my items, first or second class as applicable.

2. BPR – much the same as above but recorded.

3. CRL – used for parcels recorded or standard.

There are three main advantages of having an Online Business Account:

1. All similar items are grouped together and paid for using their average weight. For example, if I send 25 lipsticks each weighing 25g then they are all priced at the 'up to 100 grams' rate. If I send five heavier items at the same time (which are also less than 25mm thick) then the average weight rises slightly but does not exceed 100 grams, so this means I can send the heavier items at a reduced cost.

2. Using the OBA gives a discount against published RM prices. Every little helps.

3. There is no need to hold stocks of stamps. Payment terms are 30 days and you settle through your account so cash flow is improved.

Royal Mail compensation process

My view of the current Royal Mail compensation procedure for lost items is that it leaves a lot to be desired!

If a parcel is lost in the system then Royal Mail will compensate for its loss up to a set figure, which changes year-on-year. You will need proof of posting and some proof as to the original value of the item; the receipt should be fine. Unfortunately you will have to wait 15 working days from the date of postage before claiming. So far so good I hear you say, but here is where things get very difficult for eBay sellers. I will describe how the process works in the form of an example transaction.

I buy an item for £15 and my customer buys it from me for £25. If my customer then posts the item on to a friend, or whoever, then they can claim the purchase cost of the item to them – i.e. £25 – if it goes missing. If the item had gone missing when I sent it to the customer initially, as I only paid £15 for it this is the amount that I can claim. If my supplier posted it to me and it was lost then they would only be able to claim the cost to them, and so on down the supply chain.

So, in essence, you can only claim the cost of the item when you bought it, not what it was worth to you when you resold it.

Another issue is that in order to claim the cost of the item you will need a receipt, which is not the easiest thing to get at a car boot sale. If you don't have a receipt then the only other option is to ask your buyer to claim on your behalf, using the eBay invoice as a receipt, but this is not very practical and you're unlikely to take this route.

I wonder what the situation would be if you sold an item at a loss and it went missing – say you buy it for £5 and have a receipt for this, but sell to a customer at £4. Would Royal Mail then pay you compensation at the purchase price shown on your receipt? My two letters asking for clarification on this did not get a reply; I guess they were lost in the post.

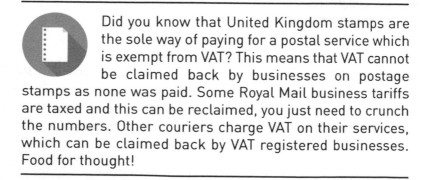

Did you know that United Kingdom stamps are the sole way of paying for a postal service which is exempt from VAT? This means that VAT cannot be claimed back by businesses on postage stamps as none was paid. Some Royal Mail business tariffs are taxed and this can be reclaimed, you just need to crunch the numbers. Other couriers charge VAT on their services, which can be claimed back by VAT registered businesses. Food for thought!

Specialised carriers

For larger parcels and for special deliveries, you may choose to use the services of a specialised carrier. They each have a range of delivery options, so you should be able to find the best service to suit your requirements. A few of the main carriers are listed in Table 12.

Table 12. Other carriers

Carrier	Services offered
Parcel Force Worldwide www.parcelforce.com	• Delivery across the UK, with next working day delivery to most locations by 9am, plus online ordering and collection. • Delivery to all European countries, with next working day delivery to most major cities. • Delivery to 240 destinations, from two working days, plus other less urgent services. • A range of same day services for parcels or documents that need to be sent urgently within the UK. • A range of worldwide road and air services. International services are guaranteed, can be tracked and offer insurance options. • Account facilities with leading carriers if your volume of packages is greater than five a day. For smaller volumes, use their 'Send a Parcel' service, which again can be tracked and has insurance options.
DHL in partnership with 'Parcel to go' www.parcel2go.com This site offers reduced rates to eBay members with prices starting at £8.99. It also provides packaging advice and the ability to print your own customs documents.	• Next day delivery to the UK. • Guaranteed delivery options to the UK before 10am and before 5.30pm. • International services.
TNT www.tnt.com TNT have a distribution network within the UK and international operations focused in Europe, Asia, North America and South America.	• An online price calculator which provides a guide price for your shipment. • Online collection booking services. • The ability to track your parcel via six different methods. • Freephone collection booking service.

Do some research and decide which carrier best suits your needs. You should check out the eBay discussion forums for real-time comments from other users.

For the rest of this section I will concentrate on the standard Royal Mail rates as they are probably what you will be dealing with most frequently.

My preferred courier

I was approached by the delivery company myHermes back in 2009, when they asked me to try their courier service. Those readers who know about me and my ways from previous editions will appreciate that I hate process changes, so I was a little sceptical.

What can I say though? This seller is most impressed! The myHermes system is easy to use, collections are flexible and delivery has been 100% (no lost parcels!), with over 1000 items dispatched so far. These guys can be cheaper than Royal Mail for certain parcel sizes but as the price tiers and costs change regularly be sure to have both sets of prices to hand. I use myHermes for almost all UK destinations, the exceptions being postcodes IM, HS and ZE.

How myHermes works

The myHermes website www.myhermes.co.uk is easy to use. You need to enter your own details just once and then for each parcel you send you will need your buyer's postcode, name and house number (just copy these from the eBay sales record page). Add these details into the form, along with the type of goods you are sending and their value. You get insurance up to £50 as standard and the package is tracked. You can pay for extra insurance if you wish.

The next step is to arrange a collection date. If you pay by 10pm it can be collected the next working day or you can drop your parcel at a nominated location and save a few pence.

In my household this means that any large parcel destined for myHermes can be put to one side, lessening the workload in the manic run up to the 6pm Royal Mail parcel run. After tea, I fill in the myHermes forms, pay with PayPal and then prepare the parcels for collection the next day. No more lugging heavy parcels to the Post Office!

 With Royal Mail rates kicking in at £5.45 for a first class 2kg small parcel (correct in April 2014) myHermes offers good value at £3.98. They score again as the weights get greater. For a 6kg parcel, for example, Royal Mail prices begin at £21.90 first class, whereas myHermes charges £7.48.

One final thought about using a courier such as myHermes instead of Royal Mail is that nowhere on the parcel will it state the price you paid to post the item. This means you will be able to charge a little more for postage with less risk of a poor DRS rating for P&P charges from your customer. With Royal Mail, as the customer can see what you paid for postage, they may be upset if you charged them considerably more than this.

When printing address labels use standard paper and your printer's quick print and black & white only options. This will save ink... and also money.

Other factors to consider with posting

Thoughts on postage charges

My personal opinion about postage charges is that the buyer should accept the overall price paid (item + postage) and not judge the seller on any excess they were charged for postage above the cost of the stamps (within reason). If the postage cost was lower then the item would cost more, equating to the same overall price to the consumer, because a seller has to make their money somewhere.

Free postage may seem like a good idea for buyers, but in fact it could end up more expensive for them when they make multiple purchases as the seller cannot combine lots and reduce postage charges as there are no postage charges to begin with.

A strange result of 'free postage' from eBay's point of view is that buyers buy fewer items as there is no postage discount for buying multiple items and so eBay lose out on any fees they may have made on the sale of additional items. You have to ask yourself why eBay would shoot themselves in the foot in this way… answers on a postcard please.

This is an area that will always be open for debate and the seller must find a happy medium between sales and customer satisfaction scores.

It is worth mentioning that applying excessive postage costs is not a good idea. Your buyers may well reflect their disapproval in the feedback they leave – they will, of course, see the amount of postage you actually paid when they receive the item if you sent it with Royal Mail. It is fair to add costs for wrapping and packing materials, and even the cost of labour, but keep it to a reasonable level.

Delivery methods

Before you can calculate postage costs, you will need to decide where in the world you are prepared to send your item and how many alternatives you will offer. As a general rule, offer first and second class rates in the UK and for overseas postage quote 'International Standard' into Europe and worldwide.

This will be three or four postage rates that need to be calculated and added into your listing. If bidders require any other options, invite them to email you and ask. If you are aiming at the TRS discounts then you do need to offer free delivery as your first UK option and also an express service (special delivery).

Exploit postage rate bands

As we have seen, Royal Mail postage rates are in fixed bands based upon the weight and dimensions of the letter or parcel. With certain items you may be able to adjust the quantity a little, or pack it in a different way, and drop postage charges into a lower band. If the item is 'fluid', such as coins, Lego or even multiple CDs, the removal of a few items may drop the postage to the previous level, making the overall cost more attractive. This will not work with all types of item, of course, but it may make you a little more competitive for some.

Also consider whether it may be possible to send the item in more than one package. This may save on postage and might also open up the overseas market. If your item is just over 2kg, for example, by dropping the weight of the main package under this level and then sending a second, smaller packet, international members may decide to bid because your postage charges will now be more competitive.

All of my items under 2 kilos are currently sent via the Royal Mail unless they are particularly large.

As mentioned previously, I have a Royal Mail Online Business Account (OBA) for my cosmetic business but my other items are still sent in the conventional way.

The basic postage services I use for non-cosmetic sales are:

- Second class post: for items up to 2kg.

- myHermes for items over 2kg or thicker than 8cm and for those that are just too big to cart to the postal depot.

- International Standard into Europe: up to 2kg.

- International Standard to the rest of the world: up to 2kg.

These are the services that I use to cover the majority of transactions, but they are not the only services available. It is possible to send items by first class post, but this is more expensive and the point of the exercise is to make the postage costs as low as possible. I have not sent anything internationally by surface mail for many years but it does still remain an option.

How will the item be packaged?

Before you can weigh and measure the item and calculate the postage costs, you will need to give some thought to the packaging materials to be used as these will add to the overall weight. Small items such as CDs, DVDs, videos, batteries, etc., will fit into a bubble bag and the weight of this packing can be taken into account.

If you can keep the thickness of your package under 25mm then depending upon the other dimensions you should be able to make use of the Royal Mail large letter rate. Try to make your parcels long and thin, keeping them within the dimensions that qualify as a small parcel wherever you can. For larger items, make an allowance for a box or wrapping and remember to add it to the weight of the item when calculating the postage cost.

Estimated time for delivery

If an item is too heavy for normal post, it may be worth noting in the description as it will take longer to arrive, or you could offer the buyer the option to pay for a premium delivery service.

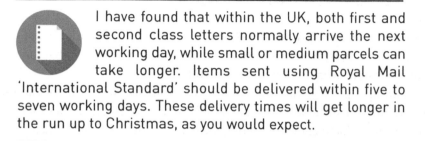

I have found that within the UK, both first and second class letters normally arrive the next working day, while small or medium parcels can take longer. Items sent using Royal Mail 'International Standard' should be delivered within five to seven working days. These delivery times will get longer in the run up to Christmas, as you would expect.

As detailed seller rating (DSR) scores for P&P are calculated using feedback from the UK and Ireland it may be worth reducing the postage costs to Ireland to encourage higher scores. Whilst the rest of Europe can still rate your charges, these ratings do not impact on your eligibility for fee discounts in the same way that ratings from the UK and Ireland do.

Five top tips for postage

1. **Keep postage costs as low as possible**. Don't leave yourself open to bad feedback by overcharging for postage. Work out a reasonable figure based on your full costs.

2. **Offer more than one option for the UK**. To become a Top-rated seller you must offer free postage and an express option at the very least. The more postage options you can offer (without creating trouble for yourself) the better, as you may encourage more customers to buy from you.

3. **State international postage options in the listing**. If selling overseas, tell your customer the appropriate shipping charges – it will save time replying to emails and help them work out the true cost.

4. **Don't underestimate the weight of packaging**. Things are always heavier than they look! Underestimating the weight of an item which sells outside of the UK could cost you serious money.

5. **Maximise your use of the postage charge bands**. Get to know the postal pricing structure and adjust your item where appropriate so that the item, when packed, is within the cheapest band possible.

Pictures of your items

In the early days of eBay, many auctions did not have any pictures at all. Now every auction must have at least one picture and it seems crazy that anything could ever have been listed without a picture.

Including a great picture of your items in your listings is one of the most important elements of a successful sale. Not only this, but it will also save you a lot of time when it comes to writing the item description; a well-taken picture will show the item more clearly than you could describe in words.

A close-up picture of the reverse of a DVD or CD, for example, removes the need to rewrite the description or track listing; this saves time and shows the condition of the item.

This section covers what type of camera to use, choosing your background, lighting the photography area and preparing your item for sale.

Cameras

Choosing the right camera for the job can be confusing as there are hundreds available. You could of course stick with your smartphone or iPad, these will perform the task just fine and will already be very familiar to you. I have to opt for a digital camera, as my Nokia 3310 is not quite up to the job. This section covers some of the basic requirements that you should look for in a camera.

When purchasing a digital camera, look for one that will be easy to use – the more facilities it has, the longer it will take to master them. (Remember how long it took you to master your video recorder!) [Ed: I'm not sure anyone can remember that far back, Bob.] If digital photography is new to you, choose a point and click model that matches your level of experience.

The following is a list of camera functions which I have found to be useful for eBay.

Close-up

The close-up function will allow you to take high-quality pictures of subjects very close to the lens. These work very well with small items, or for photographing words or instructions.

As the majority of items I sell are relatively small, I tend to use the close-up function all of the time.

Rear-view screen

The camera's rear-view screen will show the actual picture that will be taken. Just position the item within the screen and the picture will be exactly as you see it.

Flash

The flash function of a camera will produce enough artificial light to take pictures. Flash does tend to alter the colour of some items and can produce strange effects where the light bounces back from a shiny surface.

After many trials using the flash function, I have decided to improve my natural light sources as much as possible, which I feel makes a better picture. Experiment with your camera and settle on a method that works for you.

Pixel number

Pixels are the small dots that make up a digital picture. Your television screen is constructed in much the same way: the more pixels in a picture, the greater the quality of the image.

eBay have now introduced a minimum size for pictures of at least 500 pixels on the longest side and recommend that the longest side should be 1,600 pixels. Most modern cameras are capable of producing pictures that fit these specs.

Cameras are sold quoting the maximum number of pixels that pictures can have. These limits are increasing year by year, but more pixels means larger file sizes; storing these on a computer uses more space, which can be an issue if you host your own. So, the higher the quality of the picture, the fewer the number of pictures can be taken and stored on the camera at one time. As the number of pixels decreases, you can take more pictures before you have to transfer them to your computer.

Pictures that are hosted by eBay are reduced in size to fit with the standard templates, so the original size will not really be an issue.

I currently use a 14 megapixel camera. This quality level is absolutely fine for eBay.

USB connection

Although it should be standard now, ensure your camera can connect to a computer via a USB cable. This will transfer your pictures from camera to computer quickly and is easy to set up.

Memory size

Many digital cameras are sold with a very small memory capacity. This is too small to store many photographs. When buying a camera it is a good idea to buy a memory card at the same time – 2 GB or higher is recommended.

To give an idea of memory card prices and sizes available, below are a few examples from www.tesco.com. For the sake of comparison, I have also added the purchase prices that were available from eBay on the same day.

- TDK 4 GB memory card, £5.50 (£4.33, free postage).
- Kingston 8 GB memory card, £4.42 (£3.99, free postage).
- Transcend 16 GB memory card, £10.20 (£7.75, free postage).
- SanDisk 32 GB memory card, £17.00 (£7.50, £3.50 postage).

As you can see, always good deals to be had on eBay!

Cost

To give an idea of cost, but not necessarily a recommendation for specific models, here are some sample camera prices from a quick online search:

- **Olympus VG-180**. Features include: 16 megapixels, LCD viewfinder, max. resolution 4608 x 3456 pixels. £60 from Amazon (www.amazon.co.uk).
- **Panasonic Lumix DMC-XS3**. Features include: 15.3 megapixels, 4 x digital zoom, max. resolution 4320 x 3240 pixels. £119 from Argos (www.argos.co.uk).
- **Samsung MV900**. Features include: 16.31 megapixels, 5 x optical zoom, red-eye reduction. £149 from Pixmania (www.pixmania.co.uk).

Background

As you browse through eBay, look at the backgrounds that sellers use for their pictures. Some are great, and some, such as highly patterned carpets, don't work at all.

To display your item well, choose a backdrop that is clean, bright and not cluttered. Avoid strong patterns on table tops, curtains, carpets and so on. Instead, make up a temporary studio in a well-lit area. Drape a sheet over some boxes and experiment with different colours until you find something that works well and is convenient.

Try to standardise your background colours and design as regular buyers will spot your items when scrolling through search results. Far too many sellers use bland backgrounds or stock pictures and their items cannot be quickly identified against those of other sellers.

The other benefit to this is that you should be able to spot if another seller uses your picture for their item. A seller who is too lazy to take their own pictures will browse Google images and yours may pop up. From there it is easily copied. This sort of thing happens quite a lot and is not allowed – eBay will act on this if asked.

Imagine the point of view of a customer who sees two of the same item – which on the face of it are both from the same seller because the product photos are the same – at different prices. They would be confused and may be deterred from buying. I always report sellers who steal my product images and I email them requesting that they remove the picture. This note is not in my usual cuddly kind of language.

Lighting

Natural light is the best to use when taking pictures; however, this can prove very tricky during the winter months. Many sellers use light boxes or similar studio systems – these will allow you to take pictures at any time and can be purchased on eBay and at photography shops.

I use natural light for my pictures. I take as many pictures as I can on bright, sunny days and store these on my computer. By ensuring that I have a well stocked library of pictures I can list items when I wish to.

I would recommend you try to avoid taking pictures under artificial light as they do appear very dark and often distort the colour of the item. Some cameras have a setting for artificial light, which might be a solution to the problem. You should also try to reduce shadows as far as possible.

Representing the colour of your item accurately will help prevent misunderstandings with your buyer, such as the following:

- I listed an item with the description: "A super red cosmetic bag made by Clarins."

- And received this question from a buyer: "Hi, are you sure it's red as it looks pink to me??"

How many pictures to use?

Just how many pictures you decide to include in your listing will depend upon the item you are selling and how you want the overall presentation to look. You can now include up to 12 pictures for free and I would recommend you make the most of this to show as much of your item, from as many different angles, as possible.

Saving pictures on your PC

Folders

Create a dedicated folder on your computer to store your eBay pictures. This will save time at a later stage. It might be worth splitting this folder into different sub-folders for each month, so that all of the pictures for items sold during, say, August appear in the same place on your computer.

The same procedure can be used for different types of items – maybe a separate folder for DVDs, computer games or shoes. If you sell seasonal items, separate folders for the time of year might work well.

File names

When saving pictures on your computer, select a file name for each image that relates to the actual item; this will make it much easier to find later. Your camera software will allocate a unique number to each picture, which will just be a numerical reference and will mean nothing to you later [Ed: Unless you have a photographic memory].

For example, if you are selling a pair of brown shoes, it might be an idea to take several pictures; one from each side, one of the soles, one of the heels, one from the front, one of the size and brand if these are printed on the inside of the shoe, etc. Naming your pictures could be something like:

- Picture 1: brownshoes-left.jpg

- Picture 2: brownshoes-right.jpg

- Picture 3: brownshoes-sole.jpg

- Picture 4: brownshoes-heels.jpg

- Picture 5: brownshoes-front.jpg

- Picture 6: brownshoes-inside.jpg

This name format will ensure that the pictures are grouped together in your picture folder, making them easier to find and load on to eBay when you list the item.

In a later section I will discuss how to load your pictures directly into the listing, bypassing the eBay system – this may be of interest if you want extra large pictures or are not happy with the standard procedure. By using the naming convention above, this step will become much easier, too.

Format

I will discuss the various formats of files, and pictures in particular, in a later section. For now, I will just say that if you save your pictures in JPG format, you will not have any problems with eBay.

What is a JPG file?

The JPG file extension (pronounced 'Jay Peg') is the correct format for photo images that are intended to be used on websites or for email. The JPG file is compressed by 90%, or to only 1/10 of the size of the original data, which is very good for transferring between computers (e.g. loading pictures on to eBay).

However, this compression efficiency comes with a price. JPG files will lose some image quality when the JPG data is compressed and saved, and this quality can never be recovered. You can show a JPG file at smaller than the original size, but if you try and enlarge it, the quality will be poor.

Editing your pictures

Almost all digital cameras come with software that allows you to download the pictures to your computer. Often this software also allows you to edit and make simple corrections, such as adjusting the size of your pictures. Failing this, you should be able to use a standard photo editor program to alter your pictures.

Photo editing programs

There are some great photo editing programs available for free on the internet. This free software may have some restrictions, such as it may be an older version of a program or may not have as many features as the paid-for version. The company offering the free software will, of course, try to convince you to buy the most up-to-date edition, but you may not need to do so.

Check some of these websites listed in Table 13; you may find just the piece of software you are looking for and for free.

Table 13. Photo editing programs

Program	Notes
Serif PhotoPlus Starter Edition www.serif.com/free-photo-editing-software	• Serif gives away previous versions of its software to entice users to purchase the current version. At the time of writing, you could download a completely free version of Serif PhotoPlus Starter Edition. • PhotoPlus is image editing software that allows you to create, manipulate and enhance photographs, bitmap graphics and web animations – just about everything you would ever need for your eBay pictures. • All the tools you need are provided in the download, along with handy hints for some great results.
GIMP www.gimp.org	• GIMP is a popular image editor with many of the features of higher-priced programs. It is a freely distributed piece of software for such tasks as photo retouching, image composition and image authoring. • It works on many operating systems, in many languages. There may be some issues surrounding the frequency of software updates, although it does work well with Windows.
Ultimate Paint www.ultimatepaint.com	• Ultimate Paint is great software for image creation, viewing and manipulation on a Windows computer. • It was designed to be fast and compact. It can be used to retouch and enhance photos and has a set of built-in tools. • Features include resizing, rotating, flood filling and text operations.
Pixia pixia.en.softonic.com	• Pixia was originally developed in Japan and is now available in an English version. It is a free painting and retouching software, featuring custom brush tips, multiple layers, masking, vector- and bitmap-based drawing tools, colour, tone, lighting adjustments and multiple undo/redo.

If you're using a Microsoft operating system, then you may find the Paint program that comes for free, bundled with Windows, to be sufficient. This is what I use. It's usually nestled away under Programs > Accessories.

Orientation

While we are talking about editing pictures on the computer, an important thing to be able to do is to rotate your picture so that it always looks as it should. It will be difficult for a customer if they are trying to look at a picture of something on its side. This happens quite often. If the item should be seen in an upright position, rotate the picture until it looks correct.

The most pictures I have ever used was 34, when I sold a car. This auction also allowed the visitor to hear the engine running by downloading a small sound file. This unusual approach to the auction resulted in three times as many hits as similar cars were receiving.

References

Digital photography is a huge topic that would need a whole book to itself to properly explain. So treat this chapter as just an overview, with the most important points highlighted. If you're completely new to digital cameras, then the references below should help.

- www.vividlight.com/articles/3016.htm – Quite a detailed introduction to digital photography.
- www.betterphoto.com/article.asp?id=39 – How to take photos for eBay.
- www.techhive.com/article/112658/article.html – As above.
- www.imaging-resource.com – A good reference for selecting a digital camera (check out Dave's Picks in the Camera Reviews section).

Five top tips for great pictures

1. **Keep it simple**. Don't confuse your buyer with a complex picture: centre the item and focus the shot, ensuring that there are no other items within the picture area. Don't get too artistic!

2. **Have a clean background**. Choose your backdrop carefully. Erect a temporary studio if possible and ensure that the picture background presents the best image of your item.

3. **Use the best lighting available**. Avoid shadows at all costs; dark pictures do not help sell items. Consider a lighting studio or light box.

4. **Rotate portrait pictures**. It is not helpful having to twist your head round to see an item which has been photographed using a landscape picture that has not been rotated. Turn your pictures so your items are up the right way.

5. **Be aware of the item scale**. Include a scale reference within the picture, maybe a coin or ruler, just to ensure that the buyer understands how big the item is. (Especially true for rock groups buying models of Stonehenge!)

Best Match

One final thing I would like to mention in this preparation chapter is Best Match. This is the standard way in which search results are ranked when someone searches on eBay.

Buyers can opt to display search results using other criteria, too, as we have seen in a previous section. However, as most probably stick with the default option it makes sense to have an understanding of how Best Match works and how to get your listings as high up the search rankings as possible.

The basics

The first thing to ensure is that all the basics are covered. To do this you should:

- Choose a comprehensive, informative title using appropriate keywords.

- Select the correct category or categories for your item.

- Fill in as many of the 'item specifics' – such as brand, size, colour, style, etc. – as possible. eBay use this information to determine which items are most relevant to a search.

- If your item matches a product in the eBay catalogue (this will be indicated to you on screen when you are listing your item), use the details eBay provide.

Searches made for items that appear in the catalogue will be shown first in search results.

Customer Satisfaction (DSRs)

Now encompassed within the baffling Defects system, detailed seller ratings (DSRs) influence where your items will be placed in Best Match search results. The better your customer satisfaction scores, the higher up the results your items will appear. As I have described earlier, buyers rate you on four criteria:

1. Item as described.
2. Communication.
3. Dispatch time.
4. P&P charges.

Performing well in each of these areas should ensure you get a boost up the search results, and if all the DSRs don't actually contribute to the overall defect rate then you've still got a happy customer.

Buyer satisfaction ratings

In addition to the DSRs, eBay also take into consideration other customer satisfaction factors; these will also impact on your position in the Best Match results. Your rating is lowered if:

• You receive a negative or neutral piece of feedback.

• A buyer opens a dispute case against you for an item you sold that was 'not received' or was 'significantly not as described'.

Postage costs

eBay give a boost in the search results to items that offer free postage. This will also improve your DSR for postage & packing charges, so it is worth considering. Free postage is a prerequisite for a TRS and unavoidable if you want discounts on eBay final value fees.

Build on recent sales

The basic idea here is to sell more items from the same listing as all the sales are added together to boost a listing's position in search results.

eBay define recent sales as "the number of unique buyers who bought items from your fixed price listing."

How to build your recent sales

- Opt to 're-list' your fixed-price item when it sells (if you have more stock of the same item) as opposed to using the 'sell similar' option.

- Use a multi-quantity listing to sell several items at once; each sale will boost your listing in the search results.

- List variations of a product in one listing whenever you can; the listing will get increased visibility in search results as your items sell.

- Opt for the 30-day duration or Good 'til Cancelled as this will allow more time for your sales to build.

Summary

You should now have:
- Checked out the competition.
- Prepared your item.
- Got your packaging materials ready.
- Given consideration to your listing design.
- Formed your trading terms and conditions.
- Thought about how you will accept payment from customers.
- Worked out the postage methods and costs.
- Photographed the item and have the photo files stored on your computer.
- An understanding of the Best Match search.

You should now be ready to create your first listing!

But, just before moving on to that, I have listed below some things to think about that will apply to all of your listings.

Five top tips before kick off

1. **Check your competition regularly**. Trends on eBay are always changing, so make sure that you have the right items for sale at the right time.

2. **Check completed listings**. Use the 'completed' or 'sold' searches to find out how prices are holding up for items similar to those which you intend to sell. You should be able to work out a trend: if prices are falling fast, consider a shorter auction duration, a fixed-price listing or holding on to the stock until prices pick up.

3. **Be open to new ideas**. Consider any new ideas that you might come across; evolve wherever you can to keep one step ahead of the competition.

4. **Compare postage costs against your own**. High postage costs really annoy buyers and if your charges are much higher than other sellers are charging, it will deter customers. Always compare charges with other sellers and keep them as low as possible whilst covering all your costs.

5. **Research each new type of item you list**. If you start to sell a new line, check eBay to see how other sellers are listing it and compare keywords. Then adapt their listings to your own style.

FOUR

CREATING THE FIRST LISTING

Overview

This is it, the time has come to place your first listing on eBay. As with all things, it is easy when you know how!

This chapter provides a step-by-step guide to making that first leap into your online business. It contains the information you will be asked to submit, along with suggestions, hints and tips based on my 100,000 transactions' worth of experience – these will help you to drive your sales. The process is almost identical whether you are adding a fixed-price listing or an auction; I will cover any differences along the way.

The listing process has three main stages:

1. Category selection.
2. Create your listing.
3. Review your listing.

eBay will guide you though each stage with on screen directions – the listing process itself is quite straightforward. And the good news is that after you have completed one listing, the option exists to 'sell a similar item', so all of your terms and conditions, postage details and so on are retained and you will not need to enter them again.

Stage 1: Category selection

The very first step in the selling process is to access the online forms that when filled in will create your listing, displaying to the world your wares for sale. This is done by clicking on the 'Sell' link which is on the top menu next to the 'My eBay' link. If you are not already signed in, you will be asked to do so. When this screen has loaded, you will be given two choices; eBay is full of choices as you will discover. The choices in this instance are either to use the 'Quick sell' or 'Advanced sell' method.

As you might expect, the 'Quick sell' is a cut-down version of the listing process with eBay selecting a selling category on your behalf based on the information entered. If you have already registered as a business seller then the 'Quick sell' forms don't support all the options needed so you are forced down the 'Advanced' route anyway. As this book is primarily aimed at readers who will eventually run their own eBay business I will jump straight into the 'Advanced' option and this is what I describe below.

Now the process of category selection can begin!

As the final value fees payable to eBay are based on the category in which an item is placed, choosing the correct one is important. If you have a choice between two then select the one with lower fees.

Selection of category

There are thousands of categories within the eBay system and they are continually changing as products become fashionable or as trends end.

The categories work on a menu/sub-menu basis; just click the 'Browse categories' link and the main categories will be shown. The first choice is to select the main category, perhaps 'Baby', then to pick the subcategory that best suits your item, perhaps 'baby feeding', and so on until there are no more options available and you see the message 'You've selected a category. Click Continue.' If the subcategory has further options, it will have an arrow next to it and a new menu will appear.

eBay offers some help here. There is a category search engine which will suggest the most appropriate category; just type a keyword or phrase into the box on this page, maybe 'baby feeding', and the suggested categories will be shown. You can also see the last ten categories you listed items in, which might help make category selection quicker this time.

Some items can be placed into a number of categories. If, for example, your particular area of sales is pop photographs and memorabilia then you might list using the category 'Music > Music Memorabilia > Pop > Photos'. Alternatively, you could select the category 'Collectables > Photographic Images > Contemporary (1940-Now)'. Compare the fees and choose wisely.

Check on other similar listings

Another great way of selecting the best category for your item is to see what the competition is doing. Type your item into the main eBay search engine and similar items will be found; by viewing them, you will be able to see the categories in which other sellers have placed these items.

Multiple categories

It is possible to list your item in more than one category. eBay make a charge for this, but it can increase the number of potential buyers that visit your listing. Approximately 25% of all sales are made by those who browse the categories for items, so for certain items a second category could prove very worthwhile. To add your item to a second category, just click 'Add a second category' and repeat the process. Watch out for those extra fees though.

Second categories should only be used where the item logically fits into more than one. This does, however, require some understanding of what the other categories are. This knowledge can be gained by more research, using the suggested category search engine or searching for the item yourself.

For example, if you are selling a collection of Thomas the Tank Engine trains made by Brio, there is a category for 'Thomas the Tank Engine', which will contain all manner of items with this theme, and there is also a category for 'Brio', again with a vast array of items. By placing your item in both categories, your item may be found by both Thomas and Brio browsers.

No logical category?

If your item has no logical category or subcategory, then eBay do offer a final option. At the bottom of most subcategory lists is one beginning 'Other'. This is not the best place to place your listing, because people browsing categories may not find it, but if all else fails, this will work. Another place to list items that are not mainstream is in the main category called 'Everything else'.

Once you have settled on a category for your item, just click 'Continue'.

Stage 2: Create your listing

The second step is selecting the title and description of your listing, pricing information and payment details.

This is the most important part of your listing; it is where you can describe the good (and maybe the bad and the ugly) points about your item with the intention of making it irresistible to buyers. What you write here will either help the item to sell and increase the value of the bids you receive, or it could deter a visitor from buying.

Some of the shortest descriptions I have seen to date include 'See picture', 'As shown' and 'Box of toys'. This is not a recommended approach! The picture(s), as we will see later in this section, is undoubtedly the best selling aid, but do not overlook the impact that an accurate, descriptive and personal narrative can create.

It is not enough to just take a picture and submit a listing on eBay. There are so many competing items for sale that if you do attract a visitor you need to actively sell your item. The fewer negative aspects you have to mention the better your description will be. Highlight all of the positive points and sell your item as though it was your most cherished possession. For example if you have a bag of Lego weighing 700 grams but some of the pieces are damaged then take out the bad bits and sell a bag of 600 grams thus removing the need to add a negative point about damaged pieces.

During the earlier research phase you decided how your listings should look – the layout, colour scheme, font size and so on. It is within this section that we will test out those ideas and see how they look.

Extra option for eBay shop owners

I'll cover eBay shops later in the book but just to say that if you do have an eBay shop this is the place where you will be able to select the best category within it. *It's all categories so far.*

Title

The title of your listing should be considered as the doorway to your shop; it is important to have as many visitors as possible and the title will attract them. eBay have some rules about the title space, with the main one being the length of what you can type; the available space will count down from 80 with each character you enter.

The title bar has 80 characters; make use of them all with as many key search words as you can fit in. The more information you can give your potential visitors, the more likely they are to click through to your listing.

Punctuation within the title space

The space within the title section is limited and as it forms the main entry point to your listing it needs to have as many keywords in it as possible. It is therefore important not to repeat key search words.

For example, one of the most searched for words is 'toy' and also searched for is the word 'toys'. So on the face of it, a good title would have both of these words in it. eBay, however, have altered the search engine for certain words and they return almost the same number of results.

To make things a little more complex eBay have built the search engine such that the results also include items that might also be of interest and are related to the search request. All this means that there is a small variance when searching for plurals, but for all intents and purposes the search for 'toy' and then 'toys' will produce the same number of results. This is allowing for any listings that ended or began during the time it takes to complete the second search. Therefore do not waste space using both words.

This same principle also works with punctuation marks. The comma is ignored, as is the slash and the full stop, along with several other characters, so you can punctuate your title (or not) without fear of losing search results.

Keywords and phrases

 Be wary of listing fixed-price items containing phrases such as 'ideal stocking filler' or 'great Christmas gift'; these will look a bit odd at Easter.

Approximately 75% of buyers search for items as opposed to browsing for them. Therefore the trick is to get as many of the most searched for words into the listing title as possible without 'keyword spamming'. This is the annoying habit that some sellers employ to entice you to view their wares: they will include words within the title that do not relate directly to the item, but are popular search words. This practice is not allowed and may result in the removal of your listing from eBay, or worse!

In an attempt to counter the keyword spamming problem eBay have built the search engine in such a way that it ranks results based partly on a sales success ratio; the more sales per number of visits the higher you are placed in the search results. A seller using spamming words in their title will fall foul of this as many may visit but few are likely to buy so their listing falls from grace.

The top search words for each category are reproduced from time to time within eBay and by checking other similar listings you will be able to identify the keywords you should use for your items. For example, one of the most searched for words or phrases is 'new', so if your item is new be sure to include this in the title.

'In the style of'

Try and avoid using certain words which are used to place a key search word into the title. For example, if selling a mobile phone made by a less popular manufacturer, avoid words such as 'Nokia style', 'similar to Nokia', 'the same as Nokia' or 'not Nokia'. These words when used with any popular search word – such as Nokia in this case – will drive more visits to your listings, but the visitor will not have found the item they were looking for, in this case a Nokia phone. They are very likely to feel misled and are unlikely to buy.

Spelling

Check and double check the spelling of words in the title. If your keywords are spelt incorrectly then those who are searching for items and spelling what they want correctly will not find your items.

 Some of the classic spelling errors that I have made over the years include a great 'Simpsons Camra' instead of camera – that item didn't fetch very much, but did sell to a lover of real ale. I listed a super paperback by the author Terry Ratchett, which didn't get many hits and only received one bid. Even now and then I get it wrong – rushing the title section is not a good idea.

Try searching for stock items by deliberately including a spelling mistake in your search, such as Liliput Lane, with a missing 'l'. This way you find someone who has made a spelling mistake in listing their item – there are always bargains to be found with badly spelt titles. You can search for these badly spelt bargains with this great tool from auctionlotwatch: www.auctionlotwatch.co.uk/auctionspeller.html

Subtitles

Adding a subtitle to your listing can be used to provide buyers with more information and will also catch their eye as they browse down a list of search results.

Use the subtitle feature to:

- Highlight key selling points about your item (brand name, artist, designer, accessories or options).

- Provide additional information about the item that won't fit in the main title (item condition, benefits, specifications, model number, or any extras you might offer).

- Make your item stand out from other listings.

The subtitle contents are not included in the main search engine criteria, so ensure that all keywords are in the main title and supplementary information is in the subtitle.

Generally I do not use subtitles; they do of course eat into your profit as they currently carry an extra fee. But when selling a larger value item, such as a car, or more recently a collection of miniature Napoleonic lead models, they can work very well. In the case of the army of small soldiers, I sold them in 13 brigades, each with approximately 150 figures – it was quite an army! I used the subtitle to further describe the item and state which Brigade they were from. If you are using the shop format 'good 'til cancelled', be aware that your subtitle fee is three times the level of a ten-day auction listing and is charged again when the listing renews.

Top tips for titles

1. Use as many of the available characters as you can. Make the title as comprehensive as possible.

2. Ensure you use as many key search words as you can. Remember to use alternative keywords – for example, 'laptop' and 'notebook' – when describing your item as buyers may search for either or both.

3. Do not mislead your buying public. Don't bring visitors to your listings under false pretences by using keyword spamming. They won't thank you for it.

4. Check your spelling. Keywords that are not spelt correctly will not work; double check your title before you submit the auction.

Pictures

Now is the time to load on to eBay the picture or pictures you have taken and stored on your computer. This section of the form will allow you to load up to 12 pictures on to the system and the good news is that they are now all free in every category.

Fig 8. Picture upload section

There are two methods of entering pictures: you can use your own web hosting service and enter the URL (web address) of the picture or use the standard eBay picture service. Since the first of these two options is not the most common option and requires a certain level of HTML knowledge, I will focus on the standard eBay picture service in this section.

If you are selling a large quantity of items in one go, ensure your main picture shows the whole lot. Buyers may pass you by if they only see part of your lot in the gallery picture.

How to upload pictures

Fig 9: Picture upload pop-up box

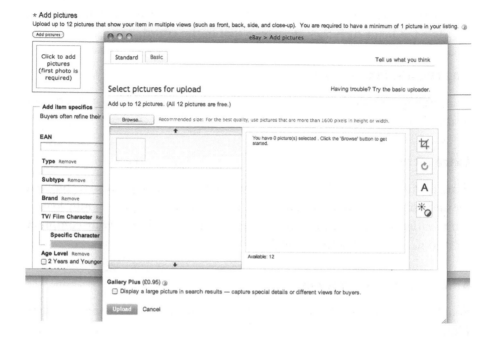

The first time you use the eBay picture uploader, you may be asked to download a small software program which allows this to take place. Then it is just a case of clicking the 'Add pictures' button and finding the pictures on your computer. This tends to be within the 'My Pictures' folder, although it could be on your desktop or any other location where you have saved the pictures. Just double click on the picture you want to use and press 'Open' or 'Upload'.

Don't use stock pictures

Stock pictures – showing a general version of the item you are selling, rather than your specific item – are only permitted for new and refurbished items or when listing books, music, movies and video games.

I would suggest you try not to use stock or catalogue pictures at all, particularly if the item you are selling is used or second-hand. Buyers like to see the actual item they will receive. Generic images that do not show the actual item you are selling will negatively impact on customer interest, so avoid them.

Many sellers use stock pictures for cosmetic lines so all the gallery pictures look the same. Pricing in this category is very competitive with many sellers pitching at the same price, so maybe a different lead picture will be enough to make a buyer click on one listing in preference to another one. My background is standardised such that my items stand out from the crowd – if you're looking for Mollybol items then they are easy to spot in the crowd.

No artwork, text or borders

In an attempt to reduce clutter eBay do not allow pictures with borders, artwork or text. Watermarks can be used to protect copyright.

Extra pictures

Extra pictures can be added for free using exactly the same process as you used for the first picture, up to a maximum of 12 (or 720 if you opt for a fully loaded multi-variation listing). Just imagine how you would feel if your computer crashed near the end of that listing!

Additional picture options

Should you wish to use it there is a picture upgrade option available – Gallery Plus.

Selecting this option will display a large picture in search results: eBay will display 400-pixel pictures from your listing in search results when buyers move their mouse over your gallery picture.

This is quite an expensive upgrade and I also find it quite annoying when large pictures pop up whilst I am searching and accidentally move over a picture.

The Gallery Plus feature is free in several categories so use it for these items if you can. The 'Clothes, Shoes & Accessories' category is one that my daughters use to great effect with several pictures of the item including label, stitching, designs and any faults.

If you use the free Gallery Plus option for an item, be careful if you then use this listing as a template for another item in a different category that does not offer free Gallery Plus. In this situation the system will retain the information and you will be charged the fee.

Additional item specifics

Most items on eBay can have some additional specifics added; these will vary from category to category and they include new/used, brand, colour, material, size, etc. Select the ones you want to include from the lists available. If it is a new item, ensure that you select this option as eBay operate a search option allowing buyers to find new items. Fill in as many of these item specifics as you can to give customers the most possible information about your item.

Description

Fig 10. Item description

The description is the main space to sell your item to any potential buyers. It is essentially a blank page where you can enter anything you feel will increase the chance of a sale. A great description should include enough detail so that the picture of your item is not actually required – the visitor should have enough information from the words alone (although the picture will help of course!).

There are two methods that can be used to enter your listing description:

1. Standard.

2. HTML.

Each of these methods has its advantages. The HTML section will be discussed in a later chapter; here we will continue with our listing using the standard method.

eBay formatting tools

In addition to a blank canvas, eBay have provided some basic tools which can enhance your description, making it easier to read, have more impact and ultimately increase the amount of interest in the item.

141

You will have seen from the research you conducted earlier that many sellers do not use these tools, they will just type one continuous block of text, often in block capitals with no paragraphs; this is not easy to read. It is so easy to make a better job of the description.

The basic tools currently include:

- Font.

- Size.

- Colour.

- Spell check.

Each of these functions will help with the basic layout of the text in your description. Just try out a few different combinations of font, text size and colour until you settle on a format that you are happy with.

There are several other useful buttons here: just the same as with any word processor, you can make your text bold, underline it, place it in italics and align it to the left, right or centre. You can also use the bullet functions to make the appearance lists easier to read.

Perhaps one of the best tips I can give is to check the spelling before you move on. Descriptions that contain spelling mistakes will suggest that little care has been taken with the listing, or even worse that you are not a reliable seller, which is not the message you want to give.

As a general rule I have settled on Arial text with a size 12 font. I use black text for most of the description and coloured text for any titles or for important information.

The final tool within this section is called inserts. These can be used for some great additions to your listing and are covered in a later chapter in more detail. However, even at this stage you can click on the 'Seller's other items' button and eBay will create a direct link to your 'Items for sale' page. You can then insert this into your listing where you want.

The same works with the 'Add to favourites list' – if you include this insert and if it is clicked on by a visitor, eBay will add your ID to this buyer's favourites list so they can visit you directly from their My eBay page.

Don't worry about how this actually works; I will expand on some areas later, but you do not need to know the technology behind the facility.

Positive language

It is important to write the description of your item in such a way that it is accurate and yet presented to ensure that viewers appreciate all the good points. It is not a good idea to hide the truth, or not to mention any damage or defects, as you will annoy your buyer, may lose money on the trade and run the risk of receiving bad feedback.

Enter as many positive points about the item as you can. Perhaps the clothing you are selling comes from a non-smoking home, or one with no pets. These things can influence a buyer's decision, so let them know. If something has been used only once – maybe you played a game only once – this will provide potential buyers with an idea of the condition.

Tell people why an item is for sale, but be careful not to shoot yourself in the foot. Selling a computer game because "it is just too hard for my son" may not encourage another parent to buy it for their son. Perhaps mention that you have an unwanted Christmas gift, or two of an item, or maybe you finished the computer game and have moved on to the next one.

When mentioning negatives, faults and damage there are ways to deal with this. The words 'but' and 'however' are great for breaking up a descriptive line and have the effect of leaving the reader remembering the comments after the word. This can be used within the description, whilst still pointing out any damage. Rather than writing:

A good DVD, enjoyable film, the case is broken.

Instead write:

A great DVD, the case is broken, but the film is full of excitement and action.

Always end on a positive note and be sure to list all of the good points.

Describing condition

It is important to describe the condition of your item. If it is new, then it is easy, but if the item has been used then using words such as 'good' or 'fair' could lead to some confusion. Good condition will mean different things to different people. Try to stay away from subjective descriptions and be accurate. Also remember that some people will place as much value on the box or label as on the item itself.

Mention any faults with the item along with any positive aspects. With a CD, for example, rather than say that the condition is good, mention the scratches on the case, but also mention that the disc itself is not scratched. The words 'as new' can result in a lot of misunderstandings as some bidders might expect things to be near perfect, while others may consider it to be 'as new' taking into account the age of the item. The term 'as new' is not allowed in listing titles for this very reason.

Use as many relevant words as possible

Searches made in 'titles and descriptions' will find all the keywords in the title space, but also any in the description. Therefore if you could not fit all the keywords into the title, enter them in the description space and buyers will still find your listing. Experience will show exactly which words to include.

Do not just include words that have no relevance to the item to drive up the number of hits; this is keyword spamming – it annoys bidders and eBay will cancel your listing if they find out.

 The use of abbreviations can cause some problems, especially if you are selling to a worldwide market – so try to avoid them. For example, the letters PAL used for a video system indicate that the movie will only work in a certain area. However, just writing that it is a PAL format may not be enough, mention as well that not all players can take this format and that the buyer must check their system for compatibility.

Describe the actual item

Try not to use standard descriptions of your item that can just be obtained from the internet. A description in your own words will make the item seem more personal. Use technical descriptions if they are available, but include only the relevant points.

Using links to other pages that contain additional specifications for the item has both advantages and disadvantages. The good point is that you will not have to write such a long description; however, the viewer may not click the link, or the link may not work and they will just move on.

If providing measurements of your item, include both metric and imperial. Some bidders – especially those in the USA – will still be accustomed to imperial measurements.

Make it personal

If you are selling your own item, describe how you used it. Mention any special aspects of the item; if it is compatible with other similar makes, tell the bidder. If you are selling DVDs or CDs, describe the mood they create: 'ideal driving music', or 'just what you need for a lazy Sunday afternoon', and so on.

Benefits not features

Rather than describe the features of your item, tell your bidders what benefits they will see from it, as this will help them to imagine it in their own home. For example, if you are selling a cot mobile for a baby's room, describe how the musical cot mobile allowed you to get baby to sleep in no time at all.

Mention other items for sale

One of the most successful additions to the description section is the ability to 'cross-sell' and 'up-sell' your items. If a visitor has reached your listing for a pair of walking boots and you are also selling a walking stick, why not let them know. You may end up with two sales or maybe sell just the second item, but the longer they spend looking at your listings, the more likely they are to buy something.

Potential buyers can check the other items that you have for sale from the menu towards the top of the screen, but this involves scrolling up the page. As they are not yet aware that you have other items of interest they need some prompting. Experience has shown me that promoting 'weaker' items in this way will increase the number of hits received and will result in higher prices and more sales.

There are several ways to cross-sell your items. The easiest is simply to mention in your description that you are also selling other items that may be of interest. Remember to mention them by name. Rather than stating:

"Please check our other great items."

say:

"If you are looking for walking items, please check out our walking stick and jacket too."

Use the insert 'Seller's other items' as described above to give customers a convenient link to your 'Items for sale' page.

 Buyers will always be on the lookout for a discount, so offer a reduction in postage for multiple purchases.

Ten top tips for the best item descriptions

1. **Use standard fonts**. To ensure that all bidders see your description as you would wish, stick to standard fonts as some computers do not have a full range of fonts loaded.

2. **Keep it simple**. Don't confuse your bidders with loads of detail that is not relevant to your listing; make your description easy to read and use colour to highlight key elements.

3. **Be accurate**. Include both good and bad points; don't run the risk of bad feedback. There are positive ways to describe faults in your item; practice with different techniques.

4. **Do not use abbreviations**. Write your description in plain English. Abbreviations that are used in the UK may not be recognised overseas and it could lead to confusion.

5. **Keep the layout as short as possible**. Your visitors will lose interest and move on if your description is too long. Do all you can to keep the listing accurate and to the point.

6. **DO NOT USE ALL CAPITALS**. Descriptions with only capital letters are not professional. In the internet world, capitals are the equivalent of shouting. They are harsh and should be avoided. Use capitals sparingly to add emphasis to keywords or phrases.

7. **Sell the experience, not just the item**. Detail the true value of your item and how it changed your life. Help your buyer to imagine owning it and the pleasure it will give them.

8. **If possible, make the listing personal**. The goal is to make every visitor feel that you are speaking directly to them. Remember: people buy from people.

9. **Restate the listing title**. Remind the buyer what exactly is included by adding a title within the description.

10. **Cross-sell your other items**. Make reference to your other listings. Use the description, hypertext links or even picture links, but make sure everybody knows about your other items.

Listing designers

eBay have created a number of patterned borders known as 'listing designers' that place a themed edge around your description. You can select a listing designer at this stage and see how it looks when you preview your listing. You can then change it if you wish or remove it altogether before the final submission.

eBay will make a charge for a listing designer unless you are using 'Turbo Lister' or if you are subscribed to 'Selling Manager Pro' – more on these two selling tools later. If it is not free, you may wish to create your own border. In a later section, I will expand on this and demonstrate how it can be achieved with only a very basic understanding of HTML code.

Visitor counters

You can add a counter to your listing at this point and there is a choice of styles. Counters will give you an idea of the number of visitors you receive. This should help you judge if you have the correct title and search words.

Selling format

You now come to the option to sell your item and there are two options:
1. Fixed price.
2. Online auction.

There is a minimum number of feedbacks required before the fixed price option can be used, so it may not be available for your first few listings.

1. Fixed price

The fixed price – or Buy It Now – option works exactly as you would expect. If you know how much you would like for the item, use this method and the buyer will be able to decide whether to purchase there and then.

It is worth mentioning the pricing structure for fixed-price items again at this point. Those sellers who do not have an eBay shop will be charged a flat fee per listing irrespective of how many items are offered for sale or the combined value of these items. The eBay search criteria mean that popular items will appear higher in search results, so if you have a large quantity of the same item to sell then fixed price could be a good, cost-effective option, because hopefully the items' popularity will push your listing up the search results.

I have now switched my main trading account Mollybol to 100% fixed-price listings and I only use auctions occasionally as loss leaders to attract buyers which I then try to divert to other listings where they can buy instantly. There are two main reasons why I have abandoned auctions:

1. Auction prices do not seem to be reaching the heights they used to and I cannot take the risk that an item will be sold below its true value.

2. The second reason is down to cost. With a high volume of listings an eBay shop makes good financial sense; fixed-price items fit well into the shop format.

Best Offer

You are able to invite a Best Offer from a potential buyer. It is exactly as you would expect, the opportunity to have a good old fashioned haggle but in cyber space. When a Best Offer is received, you as the seller can decline, accept, send a counter offer or just ignore the offer, which will expire after 48 hours.

The Best Offer process is as follows:

• A buyer makes an offer on your item.

• Within the 48-hour timescale you have the option to agree to the offer.

• If you agree to the offer the buyer is informed.

eBay are trialling a subtly different process which builds in further options for the buyer so you may come across a slightly longer haggling process. All this is happening as I write this edition so I am not sure how things will pan out; on the face of it I think it is a little too complicated but we will see. Whilst all the toing and froing is happening your item remains on sale and so others could come in to buy the item for the full price; or of course make their own offer.

With this new proposed process the buyer can make several offers to different sellers and pick and choose from those who agree to the offer. Time will tell; follow the outcome on this and other breaking news stories in my weekly newsletter.

It is possible to make an offer in excess of the asking price. Quite why somebody would do this is a mystery, but eBay allows it. The best one for me so far was a listing for '3 cute dolls' – BIN £6.49 or Best Offer. I received an offer of £8.00, which I considered for all of 20 seconds before accepting.

I include the Best Offer option on many of my non-cosmetic items, which does reintroduce a certain element of interactivity with my buyers that disappeared when I switched away from auctions. My rationale is that cosmetics are a commodity and there are so many sellers that price becomes the main buying trigger. Buyers know what's what and which product is best for them. I aim to be the cheapest in my chosen market so there is no need to haggle. My toys and to some extent DIY products are a little harder to price so I pitch a high figure and then invite offers so I can better judge the market value.

Even a low offer is still worth having as the next visitor will see that you are considering this offer. They will not know the value, but may well place a higher offer or buy the item outright as they know somebody else is interested.

If you are about to buy something on eBay from a seller who also has the option allowing a Best Offer then consider making an offer first, before you buy, as you may make a saving on the price. Even if you are happy with the BIN price, the seller may have enabled the 'automatic acceptance' of an offer over a certain amount.

For example, if an item is on sale for Buy It Now at £20, the seller may be happy with £18 and may have instructed eBay to automatically accept offers above this amount. So if you make an offer of £18.50 you will have bought the item and saved £1.50. If the seller has not enabled this service, your offer will not be automatically accepted and you can just go ahead and buy the item at £20 anyway.

Before you try it out on my items, I don't use the automatic acceptance of offers. Well, not often anyway.

An offer made in the closing moments of a listing that is set to 'good 'til cancelled', will still be valid for 48 hours; it will not expire when the listing ends and starts again.

Multiple-variation listings (MVLs)

The multiple-variation listing format is in my opinion one of the best options for listing. You can include multiple variations of your item in one Buy It Now listing, which should cut down on admin.

This listing format can save you time and money by enabling you to put different variations such as size and colour into one listing. You can even price each variation differently if you wish. Multi-variation listings are available in a host of categories.

The multi-variation listing format brings the following benefits:

- One initial fee covers the entire listing, including all variations. The final value fee still applies for each sale made.

- Cross-selling: you are showing your buyers all variations in one listing.

- Free multiple pictures – up to 12 for each variation. This is very handy as you cannot add a description for each item so several pictures showing faults, scratches, etc., can only help.

- The search ranking of your entire multi-variation listing will be determined by the sales score of the top selling relevant variant in your listing.

- If you run out of a particular variation then the details remain on the listing so when you get more stock just revise the listing and adjust the totals – all pictures and pricing will remain. Had you listed each item separately and 90 days had passed then a new listing with new pictures would be required.

- This format records how many of each variation have sold so you can better manage inventories and pricing. If every time you list a particular item it sells then raise the price; if on the other hand you keep increasing the quantity but there are no sales then a price reduction could be called for.

One of my busiest MV listings is for Thomas the Tank Engine train set spares – a pick and mix of track and scenery. It has now received over 40,000 hits.

 Don't cut corners when using the MVL format by only having one lead picture. Take a picture of each item you have so your buyers see the actual item. This is not so important for variations of the same thing such as jeans or shoes, but for similar items it can clinch a sale. I sell electric MCBs (fuses to you and me) and there are several slightly different variations of what is basically the same thing. By taking the extra pictures my buyer can check that it will fit their fuse board and it helps save me from the possibility that I made a mistake with the title – a picture is worth a thousand words as they say.

For the remainder of this section I will concentrate on the traditional auction format; most of the details also apply to fixed-price listings.

2. Auction

Starting price

The starting price for an auction is such a big subject that it could warrant a book on its own! There is no doubt in my mind that if the auction has a high start price, fewer bidders will be attracted. The possibility of a bargain will entice many to bid, hoping that they get lucky. The tricky bit is deciding at what price to start your auction.

Below, I will briefly cover some of the points to consider when setting a start price and then outline my thinking. In the end, experience will determine the starting price policy that you use and it will be different for all eBay sellers.

Fee pricing structure

The first thing to consider when setting a start price for your items is the current eBay pricing structure that is in place. As we have seen, the charging mechanism includes a listing fee which is applied when you submit your auction to the system. This listing fee will vary between private and business sellers.

Your first 20 auction-style listings in a calendar month won't be charged an insertion fee if you are a private seller and your starting price is between £0.01 and £0.99.

Currently, there is a price band of £5 to £14.99 for which a fee of 25p applies. To list the item at £15 will enter the next bracket of charges and incur a fee of 50p. In such a case it may be advantageous to start the auction at £14.99.

Psychology of an auction

Much has been written about the psychology involved when setting a starting price and it can be used to the seller's advantage. During your research on eBay, you may have noticed that a particular item is for sale in a conventional auction and obtained a certain price, but further down the listings you may find another auction with a fixed price for a lot less. Surely, you might think, the bidders on the first auction will stop bidding and just buy the item outright?

The reality is that they probably do not know that an alternative exists. Once they have found an item that suits them, they are likely to stick with it. Of course, there are other factors involved, such as the terms and conditions of each seller, but as a general rule if you can get as many bidders as possible involved early on, your auction will do well.

Another benefit of this is that a lower price will attract more visitors. The chance of a bargain, which they might even be able to sell on, will draw them in. They will not only see the item they were originally interested in, but also any other items that you have for sale and in particular any that you have mentioned within your description.

Naturally there is the danger that the item may not attract as many bids as you expect and it could sell for a low price. This could be down to many things: a poor title, the wrong product or even just bad luck. In some cases a low start price may indicate that the item is in some way inferior – a designer handbag with a 99p start price may suggest that it is a copy, even if it is not.

As a general rule I would suggest that you start your auctions at the minimum price you would be prepared to accept for the item and all you will need is just one bid. Experience will show you where it is possible to reduce the starting price in the knowledge that the item is likely to reach a much higher price.

Reserve price

The reserve price option is exactly what it says and works in the same way as a reserve at a traditional auction where the minimum price you are prepared to accept is left with the auctioneer. The item will be auctioned as normal, but if the reserve price is not met the item will not be sold. eBay works on the same principle, with the exception that if there is a reserve price on an item which has not yet been reached, then 'reserve not met' will appear next to the high bid whilst the auction is in progress.

There is a fee to include a reserve price; however, the advantages are that you create a safety net under your auction, just in case it proves to be unpopular. It could also demonstrate that you value the item highly and are not prepared to give it away; this may also encourage bidding. The major disadvantage comes when the auction ends. If the reserve price has not been reached, the high bidder does not actually take home the prize, which is very disappointing for them.

eBay have a lower limit of £50 for a reserve price and it is worth noting that the fees to set a reserve price are non-refundable even if the item doesn't sell.

Telling bidders that your item does not have a reserve price may actually encourage them to bid as they will know that if they do become the highest bidder then they will win the item.

Buy It Now option as well?

The next option on the listing is to decide if your item will have a fixed price as well as an auction start price. This allows the bidder to buy it outright for the fixed price or to start the ball rolling by placing a bid in the traditional way. When the auction is first listed, both the option to buy outright and the option to place a bid will exist. If anyone bids then the Buy It Now option will lapse. There is, as you would expect, a fee for adding this option.

With some items this option can work very well. Many bidders will not want to wait until the auction ends and would prefer to have the item that much quicker; this option gives them the opportunity to spend their money with you that little bit faster.

Start auctions low to stimulate interest, but be aware that you may end up selling at a lower price than you hoped for; it's a balancing act.

Quantity of items

If you opt for an auction format then this box will be greyed out as multiple item (Dutch) auctions are a thing of the past. If you are listing a fixed-price item, just enter the quantity here. You may decide to create an element of scarcity by listing only a couple of items and then revising the quantity as items sell.

 Before you accept an offer on your item, check to see if it is the last one on the listing. If it is and you have more, revise quantities before you accept the offer and the listing will remain active. Among other things, this means you won't lose those who were watching the item.

Duration

The next decision to be made concerns the duration that you would like the auction to run. As with everything else we have covered, the duration can impact on the final price your auction achieves.

The current options for the duration of an auction are:

- 1 day.
- 3 days.
- 5 days.
- 7 days.
- 10 days.
- Fixed-price listings can run for 30 days and shop inventory items can be 'good 'til cancelled'; however, fixed-price listings of one-day duration are not available.

Each option has its own advantages. A ten-day duration, for example, will allow your auction to run over two weekends. If it starts on a Thursday – which is traditionally a slow day for listings – it will end ten days later on a Sunday, which is generally regarded as a good time for an auction to end. Thursdays are also the most common day for eBay to run a promotion, offering reduced fees, or even a free listing day.

Seven-day auctions are the most frequently used on eBay. They are easy to track, will include one weekend and allow enough days to provide opportunity for more visits, whilst at the same time not asking the high bidder to wait too long for their item. The three and five-day auctions are also useful if you believe that most bidding occurs at the end of the auction, with maybe a little activity when the item is newly listed. This would suggest that the duration of the auction is not so important; it is the end time that really counts.

Shorter duration listings have the advantage of being near the top of search results sorted by 'ending soonest'. The more items you can get into the first few search results the more people will see them.

One-day auctions

The one-day auction is worth a little more explanation, as this can be a great duration for an auction under certain circumstances. If you have an item that has a deadline, for example theatre tickets, then the shorter auction will work. Seasonal events such as Christmas can be a very busy and profitable time for sellers; the one-day format allows you to make those last few sales before the event and catch the last post before Christmas.

Perhaps the most important use of a one-day auction is for those sellers who have many identical or duplicate items to sell. eBay will only allow sellers to list a maximum of 15 identical listings at one time and these have to be in auction format (duplicate listings at a fixed price are not allowed). If you have 100 DVDs to sell, you can only have 15 identical auctions listed each week if you choose the seven-day auction. A one-day auction will allow you to list 70 items in a week – just start another one when the first one ends.

Identical listings

With identical listings the choices are:

- Up to 15 identical auction-style listings AND
- One fixed-price listing OR
- One fixed-price multi-quantity listing OR
- One fixed-price listing with variations OR
- One auction-style listing with Buy It Now.

---

eBay will only display one Buy It Now listing per seller for identical items in search results. The item title will be a key factor used to consider whether an item is deemed to be a duplicate, so ensure that any differences in your items for sale are reflected in the listing title, e.g. 'half a kilo of Lego batch 2'.

If you try to list an item that you already have on the system then eBay will plaster a big red warning at the top of the screen (which is actually very useful, as I often forget exactly what I have in the shop).

Altering the duration of an auction can impact on the number of bids you receive. On the one hand if the item is listed for a longer period, it will gain more exposure; however, a ten-day auction may prove too long for some bidders to wait and they move on to an auction that ends sooner. There is no right answer. The items you sell and the experience you gain will ultimately decide which auction duration you choose.

 Auctions with a duration of one day can only offer PayPal as a payment method. If you try and add another payment option, you will get the following message:

"Dear Seller,

Thank you for choosing eBay.

Due to the level of disputed transactions in the 1 day auction format in which you are choosing to list, eBay is taking strong measures to protect both buyers and sellers on eBay.

To sell your item in the 1 day auction format, you must offer PayPal as the only payment method. Please sign up for a PayPal account if you do not already have one.

Thank you for your understanding and cooperation."

Start time (and end time)

Your auction will begin when you submit your listing and run for the duration you set. As the auction will end at the same time a few days later, try to start the listing at a time when you think it will be good for it to end. There is no perfect time for your auction to end; it will depend upon the item you are selling and the market you are aiming at. However, it does seem that an end time during the evening is the most favoured. For the American market, a later finish time may prove to be better, but not in the early hours of the morning as the UK and much of Europe will be asleep.

It is not possible to cater for the whole world, but it is possible to time your auctions so that they end when your target market is online. For example, if you are selling children's toys, then it might be a good idea to end the auction while the children are still awake, so that they can persuade their parents to make that extra bid. If it is a more adult item, maybe consumer electronics, then when the children are in bed might be the best idea so that the adults can concentrate on bidding without having the children around. Ending auctions between 7pm and 10pm should be a good compromise as this is fine for most UK and European customers and is just about OK for the American market as well.

 As the majority of items that I sell on auction are aimed at the family market, including toys, I have found that the best time for them to end is between 7pm and 10pm.

With a little thought it is possible to list your items in a sequence so that you make the best use of the end time of your auctions. There may, however, be a problem if you are selling several items and using the traditional method to list them; there is just not enough time to complete all your listings within the optimum window of time.

To accommodate this, eBay has the option to schedule your auction start time so that it will start at a pre-determined time in the future.

Schedule start time

Using this option, you can arrange for your auction to begin anything up to three weeks in advance. The scheduling facility also allows you to check your listings for errors before they go live.

The scheduling facility will allow you to market to specific countries around the world, without having to actually submit auctions in the early hours of the morning. The prime time for an auction in the USA might be early evening, which could mean listing the item well into the night in the UK.

Users of Selling Manager Pro are exempt from fees for scheduling listings; everybody else will pay for the privilege.

If you are selling a number of items that may appeal to the same bidders, do not list them all to end at the same time, but instead stagger them by 15 minutes or so. This will enable bidders to watch one auction end, grab a quick cuppa and switch to the next with enough time to spare. Don't rush your bidders, let them buy at a comfortable speed.

Listing whilst on holiday

The ability to schedule your listings is great if you decide to take a break, as they can start while you are away and with a little planning they can end just after you return. You can even check your email while you are away to answer questions. You may decide to stop listing a few days before you depart; it would make sense to ensure all your auctions have finished, leaving enough time for you to dispatch the items before you go away.

Top tips for choosing the best start times

1. **Schedule auctions**. Use the scheduling facility when you need to: for a small fee, you will be able to list at all times of the day and even while you are on holiday.

2. **Start auctions between 7pm and 10pm**. You can never cater for the whole world; somebody will always be asleep when your auction ends. A finish time of between 7pm and 10pm should cover most of the UK and European markets and will be late morning to late afternoon in the USA.

3. **End on a Sunday if possible**. A Sunday evening should find most people at home preparing for the new week at work. Choose a time after the evening meal and then choose the actual time according to who you are targeting.

4. **Start each of your auctions at a different time**. Leave a reasonable amount of time between auction endings to allow bidders who want to purchase more than one item to catch their breath.

5. **Avoid major events**. Be aware of key events such as major sports matches, the Oscars, The X Factor, I'm a Celebrity… or Big Brother – ending an auction in the middle of these will result in less bidding activity.

Applicable VAT rate included in sales price

The box for VAT rate is applicable for business sellers that have turnover in excess of the VAT threshold; it is likely that you will not need to complete this entry when you are just starting out on eBay.

Private buyers

As it suggests, this option allows your buyers to remain anonymous. As yet, I have not needed to use this facility. Although some of my auctions are a little odd, none demand anonymity.

Payment methods

As the title suggests, it is now time to list the payment methods you will accept. When you list a second item, these entries will be remembered by the system, so if the next item is similar, these will not need to be altered.

It is simply a case of ticking the boxes that relate to each form of payment you are prepared to accept. The current options are:

- PayPal.
- Postal Order/Banker's draft.
- Personal cheque.
- Other.
- Credit cards.
- Escrow.

We have already looked at most of these. However, I want to give a few more details about PayPal, Other and Escrow here.

PayPal

You may have more than one PayPal account, for micro-payments or for another reason, so be sure to enter the email address attached to the PayPal account that you wish the money to be paid into.

Other

The option 'Other' instructs the buyer that payment options are contained within the description; you can just write your preferred payment methods and use this box to tell interested parties to look in your description.

Escrow

Escrow is an eBay-approved third party which will hold the payment on behalf of the buyer while they inspect the item; if they are happy then payment is released to the seller. This may be of interest for higher-value items and does offer some peace of mind.

The process works as follows:

• The buyer sends payment to the escrow company.

• The seller ships the item to the buyer.

• The buyer inspects and approves the item.

• Funds are paid to the seller.

As with most things, there is a charge for this service and the fee will vary according to the amount of money in the transaction and the method of payment.

Postage

This is where you will select the areas of the world that you will post to. You can choose to sell to the UK only, or pick and choose regions of the world.

Domestic postage

You can either decide to offer the same postage rates to all UK buyers or choose not to post the item at all and offer collection only; after all, it is difficult to bubble wrap a shed!

For those items that cannot be posted, select 'No postage, collection in person only' from the pull down menu and then detail the arrangements either in the item description or in the 'payment instructions' box. eBay will include the item location as a guide for buyers; you can alter this if required.

eBay have set maximum costs that can be charged for domestic P&P in several categories including: Books, Comics & Magazines, DVD, TV & Film, Music, Video Games, Mobile & Home Phones. When applying P&P for a CD, for example, a seller can add no more than £4.50 for postage within the UK.

As many categories now have this postage restriction, a change in category might be possible to avoid this situation. For some items such as heavy old 78rpm records the rules state that postage must not be above a certain amount; this can be very costly for the seller. Select the option 'Courier: Heavy and bulky items' from the pull down menu and include your postage costs within your description.

Be aware that if you do not enter a postage price your buyer can choose to add their own figure (and hence may pay less than you wish) even if you have blocked this option from your listings.

Services and costs

As we have already looked at calculating the postage costs for the item earlier in the book, they now just need to be entered on to the system. This section is split into two main parts: the service(s) you will offer and the cost of each service. Use the pull down menu and choose up to four domestic postage options, so you can quote first class, second class, five-day courier and maybe special delivery.

You could if you wish offer your item with no postage costs at all. This might sound a little strange at first, but many sellers use this as part of their sales strategy and eBay enhance search results positioning for items with free postage, so it may be worth considering. Additionally there is an 'advanced search' option that allows buyers to find items with free postage.

If you decide to chase the elusive Top-rated seller badge – or as it is now known the 'eBay Premium Service' – then free postage as the first domestic postage option is a requirement anyway.

International postage

This section can have up to five entries; perhaps you will choose 'International Signed' into Europe and Worldwide and a surface mail option. These options can be changed from listing to listing and will need to alter according to the item you are selling. Just click 'Flat: same cost to all buyers', select your options from the menus and enter the cost for each.

You have the option to block specific countries as opposed to whole geographic areas; if you do not want to post to a certain country just select it from the exclusions list.

Did you know that the sale of unboxed, sample or used cosmetics is not allowed in Germany? If you needed to exclude Germany at this stage then you can do so, and the rest of Europe can still trade with you.

Item location

The item location will be very important for items that need to be collected. Give your buyers as much information as possible before they make the buying decision. There is an option here to enter your postcode and it is probably a good idea, given the number of people who now use satnavs.

 Consider including a location map on a separate webpage and include a hypertext link to this in your item description when selling items that can only be collected.

Buyer requirements

You have the option to impose restrictions on the type of bidders you will accept. If you want to apply these, click the link and a menu of options will appear. I currently opt to block buyers who are registered in countries to which I don't post and who have two 'Unpaid Item' strikes in the last 30 days. This is an attempt to cut down on the number of non-payers I receive.

Keep the list of buyer requirements as limited as you can because too many will restrict your potential customer base.

Returns policy

In this space you can provide details of your returns policy – you may already have given this some thought as you read through an earlier chapter. Business sellers may have additional legal obligations under the 'Distance Selling Regulations', as we have already discussed.

An example of a standard return policy might read:

"We aim to provide the highest levels of quality and service. If we do make a mistake, please let us know and we will do all we can to put things right. If your purchase is not as you had expected, just return it in its original condition and packaging within 14 days and we will be happy to provide a full refund, including the original postage costs."

Business sellers can require the buyer to cover the cost of return postage; however, this requirement must be included in the returns policy.

Additional checkout instructions

These instructions will appear in your final listing as 'Seller's Payment Instructions'. This is a great place to mention anything that you think may benefit a potential buyer. You could specify your local pick-up details, provide details of how often you post items, or anything else you can think of.

 As mentioned before, enter as much postal information at this stage as possible – it will cut down on the number of emails you receive.

My payment instructions currently read:

"Shipping costs include all stamps, packing materials, boxes, bubble bags, wrapping and so on. We promise: Fast Shipping, Top class Packaging, Great communications."

This is not necessarily what you would expect to find under payment instructions, but I am using the space to aid my sales by offering a customer promise.

Stage 3: Review your listing

After you hit the 'continue' button you will begin the final stage in the listing process. It allows you to review your listing and make any changes that might be required. eBay take the opportunity to offer additional services (for a fee), which will enhance the look and visibility of your item.

eBay recommendations

It is good to know that eBay have your best interests at heart and will offer advice on your listing. This will vary from listing to listing; you can decide whether to take their advice.

Preview your listing

Your description will now be shown as your visitors will see it. If you constructed the page in HTML, this may be the first time you see it in its full glory.

If you spot anything that needs amending, just click the 'edit listing' link and make the changes.

Make your listing stand out

You may well have already opted for a subtitle; you now have the option to spend even more money with the Gallery Plus option, unless the category the item is placed in includes this for free.

Finally, when you have checked all the details including the fees that eBay are about to charge you click the 'submit listing' button. As soon as you submit your listing, eBay will raise charges for the listing fee and any upgrades.

Although you have now listed, or scheduled, your first listing, you can still amend it and add to it while it is live on the system. Chapter 5 will discuss some of the things you can do.

Recommendations for the first few listings

- Keep your volume low. Don't get too carried away and list dozens of items all at once; there will be issues around packing and you may copy mistakes from one listing to another. Start slow and learn as you go.

- Keep it simple. To begin with, follow the basic eBay process for listing, use the standard template and learn the processes before getting too involved with advanced listing design.

- Allot time relative to the value of the item. Don't spend loads of time designing a description and layout for a low-value item. While it is important to create the right atmosphere, you must consider the amount of time it will take and balance this against your return.

- Take time to review each listing. Double check that your postage rates are correct, ensure you have selected the best category and so on.

Summary

You should now know:

- How to best select categories for your items.
- How to best describe your items in the title and description fields.
- What starting price to set.
- How the reserve price works.
- How to select the duration of your auction.
- What start time to choose.
- What picture options to use.
- How to improve the visibility of your item on the eBay search engine.
- How to set the payment and postage options.
- How important it is to carefully review your listing before going live.

Congratulations, your first listing should now be up and running!

But you're not necessarily finished yet. You can make changes to listings while they are live – which is the subject of the next chapter.

FIVE

WHILE A LISTING IS LIVE

Overview

There are several things that may happen whilst your auction or fixed-price listing is in progress; this section outlines some of them. You may receive emails asking questions about your item, or where you live, how much the postage is and so on. You may also wish to make some changes to your listing.

The number of amendments you can make to an auction will reduce if the item has received a bid, so you may not always be able to alter what was placed in the original description or title. However, as the seller you do retain control during the period that the auction is live. The options described below are likely to be the most common areas you may need to change.

Revise your item

Auction format

Once an item has been listed in auction format, it can still be revised; perhaps you need to correct errors, or add further information. The process is different if a bid has already been placed.

Before a bid

To revise your item before any bids have been placed, the best place to start is by going to My eBay.

- Click 'Selling'.
- Select the item you wish to revise.
- In the top section on the left side of the page, click 'Revise your item'.
- Make amendments as required.
- Click 'Continue' at the bottom of the page.
- Review the listing and submit revisions if all is well.

After a bid

When your item has received a bid, you can no longer edit all of the details. You will not be able to edit the title or description and the postage rates are now fixed. You can, however, still make some additions, and it can prove very useful to do so.

Fixed-price format

Multiple item fixed-price listings can be amended even after sales have been made. You can amend every aspect of your listing, even the category and title. This is a very positive move by eBay and much appreciated by yours truly who has been known to make mistakes which are not realised until sales have occurred.

The system does get confused if you want to increase the quantity from one whilst an offer is pending your response. It is not possible to add an additional postage cost for the second item and so the quantity cannot be altered. This is tricky if you get two offers for an item and would like to accept them both. The only option is to take one, re-list the item and contact the second buyer with the new item number.

Best Offer

If you have included the Best Offer option then, as we have seen, you can accept, decline, ignore or make a counter offer whilst the listing is active.

If you receive two offers for your item, counter-offer the lower one, leave it for a few hours and if the buyer does not accept you can always fall back on to the higher offer – nothing lost.

Cancelling a bid

You may be asked to cancel a bid that has been placed in error. The bidder can retract the bid themselves, but often through inexperience they do not know how to do so and within the last few hours they cannot retract anyway. If a bid has been placed in error and the bidder has no intention of completing the trade, it is in your interest to remove it as soon as possible so that the price falls back to where it was before they placed their bid. This new low price may encourage renewed interest.

 The strangest bid I have had on one of my auctions occurred during the auction of my car when I had a bid placed from a user registered in India. I had to cancel their bid. Although I was prepared to deliver the car a reasonable distance, there are limits!

You may of course decide to remove a bid because you are not happy with the bidder. Perhaps their feedback is not good enough or you have stipulated a minimum feedback score as a bidding criterion, which they do not meet. If you wish to cancel a bid, as with all things on eBay, there is a process to be followed:

• View the item in question.
• Select the bid history.
• Note the ID of the bidder and the item number.
• Click 'Services' from the top menu.
• Click 'Cancel bids'.
• Enter your password.
• Enter item number and User ID.
• Choose reason for cancelling the bid.
• Click 'Cancel bid' – note that all bids by this user will be removed, not just the highest bid.
• Email bidder to confirm the removal.

 In a similar way to bid retraction, a buyer can retract their 'Best Offer' placed on a fixed-price item. Whilst it is advantageous to have an offer as it can stimulate further interest, letting the offer remain until close to the 48-hour deadline does run the risk of having it retracted.

Ending a listing early

There may be some occasions where you will want to end your listing early. Perhaps the item is no longer for sale, it may have become damaged or the listing was incorrect and can no longer be revised due to bids being placed.

Ending auctions early will upset bidders and if it is done on a regular basis they may not visit your listings again in the future. In addition you will lose any watchers you have on your listing. Auctions should not be ended early just because the price is not high enough; it may well rise towards the end of the auction's running time. The process to end an auction is as follows:

• View the listing you want to cancel.

• Note the item number.

• Click 'End listing early' from My eBay or the help menu.

• Enter your password.

• Enter the item number.

• Click 'Continue'.

• Click 'End your listing'.

In an attempt to reduce the number of auctions ended early, eBay have now introduced a fee which will apply to all auctions listed on eBay if they have bids and are ended early. The fee will be charged based on the final item price that was bid when the auction is ended.

Additionally, sellers that remove bids and then end an auction early will also be required to pay a fee. The fee will be based on the highest bid received before the auction was ended. You can end auctions that have been active for less than 24 hours, even if they have bids, without incurring any fees. Well, it's something I guess.

Selling directly

You could of course receive interest in your item and decide to remove it from eBay and make the sale directly to the buyer. Unsurprisingly, eBay do not approve of this as they will not be able to charge any final value fees for the sale. On the face of it, this is a good idea from the seller's perspective as they will save some money by avoiding the final value fees. However, in the longer term maintaining a good relationship with eBay is worth much more.

Trading outside of the eBay system is not necessarily a good idea as it leads to a loss of protection for both the buyer and seller, and the normal feedback rules do not apply. If you do decide to accept a fixed price from a buyer whilst the auction is underway, there are two ways to achieve this and stay within the rules. If the item has not yet had a bid, pay the small fee and place a Buy It Now (BIN) option on the listing by using the 'Revise your item' process and inform the bidder that you have done so. They can then visit the auction and purchase immediately.

If the item has received a bid, the option to add a BIN price will lapse. If this is the case, cancel your listing, then re-list it with a BIN price as agreed with your preferred buyer. To deter others from buying the item, title the listing badly and they will not find it. Finally let your buyer know the new item number and they should be able to buy the item outright. Remember fees may apply when you end an auction early.

Respond to questions

Throughout the duration of the listing, you are likely to receive emails from interested eBay members who may ask any number of questions. The email from the eBay member will be sent on a form which will give you the option to respond. You can elect to add both the question and your answer to the bottom of your listing; if you do this then be careful how you word your response.

Some of the questions may seem a little strange, but smile and reply. Remember, you need the sale.

To make the whole question issue a little more tolerable eBay have given sellers the option of including answers to a number of pre-determined questions. Hopefully when a prospective buyer clicks on the link to ask you a question it will appear along with the answers. Satisfy their needs and they will not bother you further. This selection of Q&As can be found from your My eBay page under the 'Account' tab. A little way down the list is the link to 'Manage communications with buyers'. Follow this and you will be able to 'Manage questions and answers'. Enable this and create your own 'auto answers'.

You will of course still get some questions and if you spot a trend then keep a few standard replies stored somewhere on your computer and just copy and paste as required.

If you receive a question from an overseas eBay member, consider replying in their own language. I have found that this is very well received and might just encourage them to bid or buy. There are several language translators on the internet – you may already have included a link to one from your listing pages as we discussed earlier.

 I once received an email from a new eBay member which included a screen print of his bid confirmation page, which they believed I would need as proof of their bid. This page showed the maximum amount of their bid, which was higher than the current auction value. I replied, suggesting that they should not send this kind of information as it would be quite possible (although not allowed), to bump up the price to their maximum bid. There was no reply back from the bidder and in time they were outbid anyway.

First listing completed

That is your first listing completed. Now just sit back and wait for the buyers to flock in. If you have listed the right item at the right time, and you have entered the correct details, it should sell and mark the beginning of your online business.

If the process in this last chapter has worked for you, stick with it. There is no need to make things more complicated if you are happy with the results so far. However, there are some simple techniques available to help you vary and improve your listings. This might be in terms of the design of your listings (including the template you use) or the number of pictures you use, among other things. The next few chapters will show you some of the ways that these techniques can be employed and what kind of results you can expect to achieve when you use them.

I'll end this chapter with five tips for creating successful listings.

The top five tips for successful listings

1. **Create a friendly sales environment**. People buy from people (I might have mentioned this before – but it bears repeating). Create a listing where buyers will feel happy to do business; if it is hostile and threatening, many will move on.

2. **Welcome new users**. New eBay members are great, they can become very excited and will bid far more than they intended. Welcome them to your auctions.

3. **Price your items realistically**. Don't force your buyers away before they have even seen your item. Keen pricing should at least get them through the door.

4. **Keep the content to a reasonable amount**. Long pages full of tedious detail will put people off; they just will not read it. Buyers will see many listings and you need to tell them in the first few words and with your picture(s) why they should do business with you. Do not bore your customer.

5. **Adopt a consistent design format**. A consistent site design from the beginning will make your workload much easier and repeat visitors will know what to expect. Plan it well and stick to it.

Summary

You should now:

- Know how to revise elements of your item whilst it is live on the system.
- Understand what can and cannot be done before and after the first bids on auction listings.
- Know how to cancel a bid.
- Know how to end a listing early.
- Understand why it is not a good idea to sell direct outside of eBay.
- Know how to reply efficiently to email questions.

Even though I've now sold over 100,000 items on eBay, I still find the closing stages of auctions exciting! Will the price surge in the closing seconds…?

After the auction has ended or your fixed-price item has sold and the excitement of the sale has subsided, there is work to be done. We will move on to look at this in the next chapter.

SIX

AFTER A LISTING HAS ENDED

Overview

When a listing ends, several things will happen almost at once. First, you will receive an email notifying you that the listing has ended and whether the item sold. If it sold the buyer will receive an invoice informing them that they have made a successful purchase. Several aspects of the listing will also change and you will be able to view the particulars of the trade. You will now be able to see the buyer's email address and they will be able to see yours. The email that the seller receives will have the option to send information to the buyer. It will also have links to the item and a summary of the final details, including an option to send an invoice.

The buyer will receive an email that also includes a summary of the trade. This will contain a link to pay immediately or request more information from the seller.

How things progress from this point will depend upon how the buyer intends to pay and how quickly they respond; they may of course be interested in more of your items and continue buying.

The main point is that a contract has been agreed between the buyer and seller and as long as the buyer has all the necessary information, payment should be the next stage.

Second Chance Offer

If you have more than one of a particular item available the Second Chance Offer facility will allow you to make a direct offer to sell these items to any under-bidders in a completed auction. The seller can make an offer to any of the losing bidders if their bid price is considered to be high enough and, of course, if you have sufficient stock.

How it works

This offer does not incur any listing fees, but the final value fee will still apply if an under-bidder accepts the offer. All the details of the original auction still apply, so this option only works if you have more than one identical item. The under-bidder will receive an email containing the offer, which includes instructions on how to accept it.

The offer can remain active for a number of days, which you can decide. If you want to re-list the item soon, only make the offer valid for one day; if you are not in a hurry to re-list, extend the offer for more days.

When to use it

If any of the under-bids are at or above your expected price for the item, then the second chance option is a great way to increase your turnover. It will also remove the need to place a separate listing for the extra items.

 Second Chance Offers that are made immediately after the auction ends are more likely to be taken by the bidder. The second and third placed bidders may only just have been outbid, and given the chance they may well accept, whereas over time their interest in the item will fade.

Receiving payment

This is the best part of having your own eBay business – watching the money roll in!

Payments will arrive in the manner that you stipulated in your payment options section and the chances are that it will be via PayPal. You may, however, find that you receive payments in a variety of methods you did not expect and these may even be in different currencies.

The more payment options you offer the more processes you must have in place to cater for them. If you accept personal cheques, it is worth contacting your bank and agreeing a limit as to how many you can clear through a personal cheque account. Business accounts are almost certain to incur a fee for clearing cheques. I am not sure how many cheques will be used in the future as electronic payment is increasingly the way buyers and sellers are going, but there is no harm in giving them some thought.

It is prudent to allow any form of payment to clear before sending the item. Cheques and electronic cheques (eCheques) do take several days to clear.

The easiest way to find out if someone has paid is via the £ sign next to the item within the 'Sold' section of My eBay. When payment has been received this £ symbol changes and becomes darker so you can see at a glance who has paid.

If you do receive an eCheque through PayPal contact your buyer and let them know that you will post when the payment clears; PayPal provide an estimate of this on your notification. It is possible that the buyer may not know that they have paid in this way, so your note will go some way to explaining why they will have to wait for their item.

In the past I tended to send all items on receipt of payment; I did not wait for funds to clear. This is no longer the case and I now will not send anything until the money is safely tucked up in my account.

Late payment excuses

Not surprisingly, payment doesn't always come in quickly and smoothly. You have to be flexible. Some of the excuses I've received are:

"I am sorry, I didn't realise that I had won the auction."

"An in-law placed the bid and has now died."

"Sorry, I didn't realise you are in the UK."

"Sorry for the late payment, there was a power cut and I couldn't check my email."

But my favourite excuse is:

"Sorry for the late payment, I was stung by a wasp."

I will spend more time on non-payers a little later as they are one of my pet hates.

Packaging

Packing your items for shipping can be a tedious job and as your turnover increases it will become worse. If you gave some thought to the packing before you listed your item, you will already know how it will be packaged and you should have the materials to hand.

Only pack up the item after it sells and you receive cleared payment, as buyers quite often purchase more than one item. You do not want to unpack your box in order to include something else.

If you sell the same type of item all of the time then the packing will not require much thought. For example, if you sell lots of DVDs, you may find that a standard bubble bag will cater for up to three discs and one parcel is much like the next. If you sell a range of items of differing size, you will have a more interesting time. You may even end up making your own boxes!

It makes sense to put clothing inside a plastic bag, which might just keep out the worst of the weather, and then in a box or bubble bag.

Visit this handy site to find out the abbreviations for UK counties, it will save you time when writing address labels: www.langscape.org.uk/about/CountyAbbreviations.html

Overseas parcels

Sending parcels overseas is much the same as sending them in the UK. The actual packaging should be the same, although it might be an idea to use better adhesive tape if sending by surface mail as the package needs to stay in one piece for longer.

The main differences are in the information required on the parcel. If you are using an international carrier for large parcels, they will have the necessary documentation; if using the standard Royal Mail services, a few simple additions to the package will be sufficient.

When using the Royal Mail the item will be a 'small packet'. Just write this in the top left corner and, if sending by airmail, use a blue 'Airmail / par Avion' sticker which is available from the Post Office for free.

For parcels being sent outside of the EU, a customs declaration is also required. These are now white stickers. The information on this sticker includes the weight, value and a description of the contents. You will also need to sign and date the declaration. Be aware that not all countries in Europe are in the EU – you will need a customs label when sending to Switzerland, for example.

Multiple purchases

If your buyer purchases more than one item it makes sense to send them in one parcel; it saves you time and money and could possibly save the buyer a little on postage costs. Check with your buyer that is what they would like to do as the delivery time may increase if the larger package is to be sent in the UK by parcel post or by a courier such as myHermes.

When refunding excess postage charges, wherever possible use the refund process within PayPal as you will also recover some of the original fees on the payment.

Five things to avoid when packing

1. **Don't allow fragile items to touch other contents**. It sounds like common sense and it is. The hassle that broken items can cause is amazing, particularly if they are expensive. Use extra bubble wrap to make sure they travel well.

2. **Don't send items without the full address, including postcode or zip code**. If a parcel can get lost, it will, and it so often seems to be overseas. Some international addresses are quite complex and we are not used to the format; get as much information about the address on to your package as possible.

3. **Don't use cheap adhesive tape.** Some parcels may be in the system for some weeks and it has been known for them to start to come apart. I now use a better quality tape for certain destinations!

4. **Don't allow items to move within the packaging**. Use the correct packaging for the item and make sure it is secure.

5. **Don't use inferior or damaged packaging**. Avoid cutting corners with your packaging materials. Lightweight boxes and inadequate quality packing could cost you money and the goodwill of your buyer.

Dispatch

Sending your parcels can also be a time-consuming process. Queuing in the Post Office is not a good use of your time. Instead, see if your local postal depot will accept parcels, or, if you have a sufficient quantity, it may be worth arranging for them to be collected. Parcels sent by most couriers are usually collected, which will save a journey but could mean getting up early in the morning – myHermes usually collect from me at about 9am, which I consider to be an early start.

 To save time when dispatching, consider buying postage stamps directly from Royal Mail then weighing and stamping your own parcels before dropping them off.

Proof of posting

When using the standard Royal Mail service, you can fill in a certificate of posting (proof of postage to you and me), which confirms that the item has been sent to the correct address. It is also date stamped by the issuer. This certificate is free and, if the parcel is lost or damaged, it will help any claim for compensation. If paying over the counter for your postage the counter staff will print a certificate of posting if you ask; however, local depots no longer provide this service.

It is worth mentioning again here that a certificate of posting is not enough if you become involved with a PayPal dispute – they require proof of delivery, such as the package being signed for.

Notify buyer

When the item has been sent, click the small parcel icon box in the sales record and eBay will send an automatic dispatch notification to the buyer. When marked as 'dispatched' the icon becomes darker in colour and is also shown in the buyer's purchase history. A more experienced buyer will see at a glance that the item has been sent.

You could decide to send the buyer an additional email informing them that their item is in the post and giving an idea of how long it should take to arrive. Use this note to thank the buyer for their custom and invite them back to your site. This can be a bit of a pain if you are a volume seller and I usually just rely on the eBay automatic email.

Create your own 'with compliments' slip and include it inside your package. I now get these professionally printed, 10,000 cost £84 delivered, well worth it. If you want to see what my printer can do for you, drop them a line – richard@bluestarprintsolutions.co.uk. Mention Molly and I might end up with a free calendar at Christmas.

To cut down on time when sending these emails, write a standard note and save this on your computer. Copy the text for each email like this that you send – just change the item specifics.

Re-listing an unsold item

Some of your items may not sell; maybe your price was too high, the item was not listed correctly, or for one of many other reasons. eBay would obviously like you to sell the item so that they can charge you the final value fee, so they will allow you to re-list your item and will not charge the normal insertion fee.

You can re-list an unsold item only once for free; if it doesn't sell the second time around, you will have to pay the standard listing fee to list it a third time. This opportunity to re-list for free does not apply to fixed-price items. There are quite a few restrictions before you can qualify for the free insertion fee; check out the details here – sellercentre.ebay.co.uk/selling-fees. You would almost believe that eBay didn't really want to let you off the second insertion fee after all!

To re-list the same item again for the same price and with the same description, simply go to your My eBay page and click on the 'Unsold' link. There will be a re-list option to the right side of the page, click this, scroll down the page and click 'Submit listing'.

You can, however, change almost every aspect of your auction by using the 'edit' links before you submit. As it did not sell the first time, it would probably be worth changing something: maybe the title, starting price or even the day that the auction will finish. In order to qualify for the free listing entry, the start price must be equal to or less than the price it was the first time.

If you decide not to re-list the actual item that didn't sell, you can still qualify for a free re-list and sell a completely different item. Just change all the details of the auction, ensuring that the start price is the same, or lower, than the original item.

Non-paying buyers

Sometimes your buyer will not complete the trade and will not pay for the item, for whatever reason. These are known as non-paying buyers or non-paying bidders. As the trade did not complete, it is not right that the seller should still pay the final value fee. eBay have a process which will allow the seller to reclaim these fees and at the same time issue a warning to the buyer who didn't pay.

The reasons for non-payment vary and the eBay process will allow you to select the best option as to why the trade did not end with a satisfactory conclusion.

Claiming back fees

How long you decide to wait for payment may depend upon the type of item, where the buyer is in the world, how much feedback they have, or the policy which sets out your payment timescales. If you have hundreds of a particular item then you may be more relaxed as you have plenty more for sale. If it is a one off then you will probably want to sort it out quickly and re-list.

About 1.5% of my buyers don't pay. In each case I reclaim my eBay fees, even if it is just a few pence.

The non-paying buyer (NPB) process has one main objective for a seller: to claim back your final value fees from eBay. During the process, the buyer or high bidder will be sent an email reminding them to pay and telling them of the consequences. Often this note from eBay will prompt them into paying, so it is definitely worth sending.

If your buyer still does not complete the trade they will be given a warning from eBay – strike one. With three of these warnings their account will be suspended and they will become NARU (not a registered user) – strike three and you're out. If the person has a high feedback score then having their account closed is usually a good deterrent as they will have to start again with a new account and zero feedback.

If your buyer has become NARU since buying your item you should be able to reclaim your fees straightaway. It is possible to automate this process and let eBay send reminders – you can activate this from the Unpaid Item Assistant section within 'Site preferences', which can be found under the 'Account' tab in

My eBay. I don't use this facility and still prefer to chase up my non-payers manually.

I usually wait until one week after the sale (the minimum period is two days) and if I have not heard from the buyer I will send a polite email asking if all is OK and offering assistance. They may have forgotten about the item or be on holiday, so I give them a gentle reminder. If another week passes with no contact I will begin the non-paying buyer process (NPB). In the run up to Christmas I do start the ball rolling after four or five days as I want to get the item back on sale as quickly as possible. In order to reclaim your fees you must act within 32 days of the sale.

The NPB process is as follows:
• Start at My eBay.
• Click 'Sold items – awaiting payment' and open the item.
• Note the item number.
• Select 'Resolution Centre' from My eBay.
• Click 'I haven't received my payment yet'.
• Put the item number into the box.
• Click continue. If this is a multi-item, fixed-price listing, select the buyer's user ID.

The buyer will be sent an email reminder. They can then respond to the reminder, or pay, or do nothing. You can log in to view your disputes at any time and you will be prompted by eBay if your action is required. You also have a shortcut to this process from the list of actions located to the right of your item in the 'Awaiting payment' section.

There are three outcomes to a disputed trade:
1. The buyer pays for the item. Both parties are satisfied and the dispute is closed automatically by eBay. You will not receive a fee refund and the bidder will not get a non-payer strike.
2. The buyer does not respond and after a period of time you decide not to wait any longer and close the case. You will receive a refund of your fees and the buyer will receive one non-payer strike.

3. Both parties decide not to complete the transaction for whatever reason. When the buyer confirms this to eBay, you will receive a refund of your fees and they will not incur a non-payer item strike.

If the seller files an unpaid item dispute against a buyer, any negative or neutral feedback left by that buyer will be removed if the buyer does not respond to the dispute before the deadline, and the buyer receives a strike.

When a member is suspended, eBay will remove any neutral or negative feedback left by that member.

The Resolution Centre can also be used to cancel a transaction by mutual consent; the process is much the same as above. The link is on the right side – 'The buyer and I agree to cancel a transaction'. Enter the item number, select the reason why and then you have completed your side of things. The buyer just has to agree and the trade will be cancelled.

Buyers can also report a problem or request a refund via the Resolution Centre. It is worth mentioning at this point that as a seller you do not have to respond to a buyer's dispute in the way suggested by eBay. If, for example, your buyer requests a full refund then the Resolution Centre will present you with the option to issue that refund; but you can instead select another course of action from the available list, maybe to send a response and not the refund – don't be led by eBay.

Buyers' options are on the left side and are:

- I haven't received it yet.

- I received an item that does not match the seller's description.

Summary

You should now know:

- When to make a Second Chance Offer.

- It's better to wait for payments to clear before dispatching items.

- How best to package your items.

- How to send packages overseas.

- How to re-list unsold items.

- How to claim back fees from eBay.

- How to deal with a non-paying buyer.

Hopefully, you've now sold and posted your first item. In the next chapter we will look at ways to improve the format of your listings to make them more attractive to buyers.

SEVEN

REFINING YOUR LISTINGS

Overview

The basic listing format that we have discussed has introduced you to the mechanics of eBay and demonstrated how an item is placed on the site.

You may now have some ideas of how you would like to improve things. Perhaps you have seen other listings with imbedded pictures, or links to other pages.

The extent of any changes that you choose to make is down to personal choice. These changes can be made using HTML, or by using the more traditional standard method of listing.

This chapter builds on the basic foundations of a listing and shows some of the ways that you can make changes. Experiment with some of them: if they work for you, great; if they are not what you had in mind, then just revert back to the standard method.

Standard method

Improving the look of your listing does not necessarily involve complicated technical knowledge of computers and HTML code. There are several things that can be done just using the copy and paste functions, and a few simple codes which are shown below. It must be stressed that if you are happy with the way your listings look stick with it; only refine them when you want to achieve something a bit different.

First, we will look at two computer techniques that can make your life a lot easier.

Two tips

1. Copy and paste

To effect these changes to your format, you will need to master the copy and paste functions on your computer. If this is new to you, these few lines should help (note: this applies to Windows, but a similar technique also applies for Macs and other systems).

The basic operation of copy and paste involves three stages:

1. Highlight text. Identify the text that you would like to copy. Highlight it by placing your mouse at the beginning of the text, then hold down your left mouse button and drag your mouse to the end of the text, and then release the left mouse button. The text should now be highlighted.

2. Copy the text on to the clipboard. Hover your mouse over the text and click your right mouse button. A pop-up menu will appear, from which you select 'Copy'.

3. Paste the text where you want it. Select the new location where you would like the text to appear, click the right button again in this space and select 'Paste'.

Practice with this until it becomes easy and you will then be ready to make some design changes to your listings.

References

www.webmasternow.com/copyandpaste.html

2. Opening a second browser window

There are many situations where it is useful to open more than one browser window. For example, you might be reading a long article on Polish needlework when you want to quickly check the latest sports scores. You want to look at the BBC website to find out the score, but you don't want to lose the fascinating stitching article. This is where opening two browser windows can be helpful.

There are two simple ways to open two (or indeed multiple) windows:

1. If you are reading a web page and you want to click on a link, but you do not want to lose the current web page, hold the 'Shift' key down while clicking on the link. Hey presto, a new browser window will open, with the linked page loaded in it.

2. If you want a new blank browser window, from the top menu bar select File > New > Window. A new window will open and you can input any URL (internet address) you want.

Having opened two or more browser windows, you can switch between them either by clicking the tabs in the task bar or pressing the keys Alt and Tab.

My listing design has changed many times over the years and will certainly do so again in the future. For now, I have settled on a standard format which consists of:

- A border around the description.

- A plain, single-coloured background.

- Hidden notice boards within my description (read on for more detail).

- A link to additional web pages which contain my details and trading terms.

I feel that using links for additional information leaves the listing uncluttered and makes it easier to read. The border around the listing gives an element of continuity as I also have the same design on my shop front. As the seasons change, so I alter the look of my listings, with a Christmas or Easter theme, or maybe just when I feel like something different.

Another change I have incorporated into my listing design is to include three hidden notice boards which I can populate with messages if I wish. For most of the time these are the same colour as my background and therefore invisible. Messages concerning delays to shipping, holiday dates and special offers can be loaded quickly into this space and will appear on all past and current listings.

Inserts

We discussed the use of inserts in an earlier chapter when we used them to add the standard eBay inserts of 'Seller's other items' and 'Add to favourites list'. It is possible to create your own inserts; eBay allow up to five personal inserts to be created.

These extra inserts can be used for, among other things:

1. Terms and conditions for multiple products.

2. Standard signature.

3. Links to other eBay pages.

4. Links to external web pages.

5. Links to externally hosted pictures.

These are explained in more detail below.

The list of insert types is very long, but we will only concentrate on these five as they are the ones I feel have the most benefit and will give a good indication of how this facility can be used. The process is very similar to the one we have already used: when you are creating a listing just click on 'Inserts', then 'Create an insert', which will open in a new window.

Name your insert something relevant so you can recognise it in the future and then write the HTML code or text that you wish to include. You have a maximum space of 1,000 characters. Then just click 'Save' and you will be able to enter your insert into the item description wherever you wish.

To start with, just test the process and see how it could work for you.

1. Terms and conditions for multiple products

Perhaps you sell three different types of item, with each one needing a separate summary of trading terms, delivery times, packing details and so on. Just create three inserts and call them 'Product A terms', 'Product B terms' and 'Product C terms', then enter the specific details for each and just select the insert you need for the listing.

2. Standard signature

In much the same way as the above, you could use an insert to create a standard signature that could be added anywhere within your item description.

3. Links to other eBay pages

Links to other eBay pages can be included using the inserts facility. It involves a very basic use of HTML code. You do not need to understand how it works if you don't want to – just copy the code written below into the insert box and name it 'eBay home page':

```
<a href="http://www.eBay.co.uk">eBay home page</a>
```

This simple code will place a link in your description which will read 'eBay home page'; it can be clicked by the visitor and will take them to the eBay home page. I should not think that many would find this a tempting link and it will not really improve your sales; however, if the insert directed them to your eBay shop, or to another of your listings, or maybe to the eBay registration page which might encourage newbies to register and buy, then maybe it would be worth trying.

All that has to be done is to amend the HTML code shown above. It has two sections:

1. The text you would like to show in your description that can be clicked on (e.g. 'eBay home page').

2. The address of the page you wish to send the visitor to (e.g. 'http://www.eBay.co.uk').

In the example above, 'eBay home page' is the link text that would appear on the web page. Just replace this text with 'My great DVD auction' (or whatever you are selling at the time). The address would then need changing (in the example it is 'http://www.eBay.co.uk').

A simple way to replace the address is:

1. Open a second browser window.

2. Load the target page you want (e.g. the web page of your DVD auction).

3. Highlight the address of the page (this appears in the location bar of the browser window) and copy this to your computer's clipboard.

4. Switch back to your original browser window and paste the address in place of 'http://www.eBay.co.uk' in the code.

5. Give the insert a new name (e.g. 'DVD auction') and it is ready for use.

The first time you do this it will take a while, but you will quickly pick up the technique and if you have many items that you wish to promote this is the way to do it. Experiment and see if it works for you.

4. Links to external web pages

In much the same way as above, it is possible to create links to external web pages. eBay have rules that govern the use of links from your listings. For the full list of rules, visit: pages.eBay.co.uk/help/policies/listing-links.html

The main use for this external linking is to link to an extra page that contains further details of the item for sale. If, for example, you are selling a car, the detailed description could be quite long, especially if you want to include a number of extra pictures. The length and complexity of your listing could put off some buyers. Consider instead a standard description, with maybe a couple of embedded pictures, and then a link to an extra web page containing your detailed description.

This technique does require additional web space, which you may have from your ISP, or you may get by subscribing to a hosting company.

The method is the same as for 'links to other eBay pages', just include the address of your extra page between the two sets of quotes. For example:

```
<a    href="http://www.yourname.f2s.com/eBay/car.htm">More
details</a>
```

You can create links to currency converters, language translators and even the parcel carrier sites by following this method. For example:

```
<a    href="http://finance.yahoo.com/currency">Yahoo    currency
converter</a>

<a    href="http://babelfish.altavista.com/babelfish/tr">Babelfish
language translator</a>
```

5. Links to externally hosted pictures

This facility is one of the most interesting enhancements that can be made to your listing design. Instead of just the 12 standard-size pictures hosted by eBay you can have as many extra pictures as you want – which can be as large as you like – with no extra charges. These externally hosted pictures do not have to fall in line with the eBay pictures requirements, so you can have text within the picture.

Traditionally, linking to extra pictures in this way has only been possible with an understanding of HTML. However, it can be achieved by using the copy and paste functions and the inserts facility, which we have already discussed.

There are several hosting companies on the internet which will allow you to upload your pictures for free. For example:

• Photobucket: www.photobucket.com

• Tinypic: www.tinypic.com

These companies will allocate you an amount of web space for storing pictures. They do not charge for this service, and, once loaded on to the site, pictures can be placed inside your eBay listings.

There is likely to be a restriction on the amount of bandwidth that can be used to view your pictures. When you create a shortcut to a picture within your listing, each time the page is viewed the internet browser will contact the host server and display the picture. This process uses up bandwidth at the server end (which they have to pay for). The more people that look at your pictures, the more bandwidth is used.

Photobucket will allow a certain amount of bandwidth in any one month. If exceeded, they will disable the linking facility, which is something that I discovered to my detriment once. You can check their current terms and conditions on their website.

I cannot go into great detail about the process of opening an account with every free picture hosting company as there are so many, including dozens that I do not even know about, and each may have a slightly different way of operating. However, once created, the process of loading a picture to their site is exactly the same as that used for the eBay pictures: you just browse your computer for the picture and then upload it.

I will describe the process with Photobucket in more detail to act as a way of illustration.

Photobucket

The process to open an account with Photobucket and use it to host your images couldn't be easier. Just put the kettle on and follow the steps below.

Visit www.photobucket.com and click on the 'Sign up' link. You will need to create a username (most people just use their eBay ID), and enter the usual personal details. A confirmation email will be sent; follow the instructions and your account will be active.

When you log in to your account you will see quite a few advertisements (which is how Photobucket is funded) and a picture upload section that resembles the one used on eBay. The first thing to do is to load a picture from your computer. As with eBay pictures, just click Browse, locate the picture on your computer and click Submit. Photobucket will now copy the picture into your account.

 If you are going to use lots of pictures, create a number of sub-folders to make finding them on Photobucket easier. I file my pictures in sub-folders for the month and then additional sub-folders for the day within the month.

Once you have loaded a picture into Photobucket it is ready to be used in your eBay listing – there's just one small line of HTML code to copy and paste. Associated with each picture are with a number of HTML codes. They will look like a foreign language if you have not seen HTML before, but it is not important that you know what they mean at this stage. You are looking for the code that looks something like this:

img.photobucket.com/albums/v260/youruserid/yourpicture.jpg

Once you have copied this code, it can be pasted into eBay. This is done at the 'Titles & Description' stage. This section of the eBay listing is where you will describe your item. As we have seen, this can be done via a standard method using the inserts function or you can choose to enter your own HTML.

If you select the HTML option, you will see your listing in HTML format, which can look very daunting. Trial and error will determine the best place to paste the codes and load in your picture. There is a lot more detail on HTML following shortly, so read on to find out more about this.

Pictures

Here are some things to consider when adding pictures directly into your item description.

How big should my pictures be?

When using the eBay picture service, pictures are edited into the available space on the system. If you choose to load your own pictures into your listings, you can decide how big they will be.

 I have found that a picture size of 640 pixels by 480 pixels fits into a standard computer monitor screen. Anything bigger would require a horizontal scroll bar to see the whole picture – which you want to avoid because the secret is to get the visitor to do as little as possible.

Remember: large pictures may mean that some buyers may not be able to see the whole picture if their computer monitor is old or small.

A picture's resolution refers to the number of pixels, measured horizontally and vertically, that a computer monitor uses to display text and graphics on the screen.

The most common screen resolutions used on computers are:
• 640 by 480 pixels (only used by old or small computers).

- 800 by 600 pixels.
- 1024 by 768 pixels.

A 640 by 480 picture would completely fill a screen of the same size, but appear smaller within a larger screen.

If you load your pictures into your description at a size of 1024 x 768 pixels and the viewer has a screen size of 800 x 600 pixels, they will not be able to see the whole picture on their screen.

 If you are loading images to your own web space, edit the size of them before uploading. This will save on web hosting charges as you will be able to store more pictures.

Picture location

Each picture you store on the internet will have a unique address, which pinpoints exactly where it is. Using this address (or URL) we can include it on our item page by using a small piece of HTML code:

```
<img src="the address of your picture is in here">
```

For example:

```
<img src="http://www.yourname.f2s.com/eBay/photos/car.jpg">
```

As before, you do not need to know how the code works; it might take a little practice but once mastered the same process is used over and over again.

Loading your extra pictures into the listing

Before we can load the extra pictures into a listing, it helps to have two browser windows open: one showing the item description that you are working on and a second with the free picture hosting site, so that you can see the picture you need.

To load your extra pictures into the listing, you will again use the inserts facility and, as before, you will create an insert. Name the new insert 'Picture' and copy the code below into the text space:

```
<img src=" ">
```

You now need to place the URL of your picture between the quotes. This begins 'http' and ends with '.jpg'. Just copy this from the hosting site and paste it into the code. Now click 'Save'.

GIF and JPG are the primary file types for pictures used on the internet although you may also see some PNGs. A picture's file type is given at the ending of its file name – you will see .gif, .jpg or .png.

On the item description page, decide where you would like to add your picture, click inserts and then 'Picture' and... your picture will appear! Your new picture may appear to be huge, as there is no restriction on size. If this is the case then it is too big and you need to edit it and then reload it to the hosting site.

Remember, even with additional pictures, load pictures into the eBay system as normal. The first picture you add will be used as the gallery image and will be shown in search results so ensure you choose the best one for this.

To load a different picture, open the insert called 'Picture' again and replace the address of the old picture with that of the new picture, then save. Now when you add the insert to your description, the second picture will appear.

If you have saved your pictures with the naming convention we discussed earlier in this book, you will only need to change the last part of the file name when swapping one picture for another one. For example:

- Picture 1: brownshoes-left.jpg

- Picture 2: brownshoes-right.jpg

- Picture 3: brownshoes-sole.jpg

Your own HTML

Warning: Writing your own HTML code is not difficult, but it may look a little scary when coming across it for the first time. Take it at your own pace; your knowledge will grow as you go.

The previous section showed how it is possible to load links and pictures into your auctions using just a little HTML code. This is very useful, but the method is quite limited. Entering more advanced HTML directly into the listing can produce some great designs.

You could decide to load in small pictures of other items you are selling, I'll cover this more in a while. You also may want to add animations, videos, sound bites or pages of technical data. The principles are much the same in each case so buckle up and enter the world of HTML with an open mind.

HTML codes

I cannot cover all of the elements of HTML code here – the subject is huge. I will instead provide a few simple codes that can be used in item descriptions. Hopefully these ideas will encourage you to learn more and experiment with HTML over time. There are some great free resources on the internet that can teach you more.

The codes in Table 14 are the codes I shall be explaining in more detail over the next few pages. Don't worry too much about them now, take things slowly to start with and have a read of the table to get used to the terms.

Table 14. Basic HTML codes

HTML code	Description
<p>	Inserts a paragraph break between pictures or text.
 	Moves your text or pictures to the next line.
<center>	Places your picture or text in the centre of the page.
</center>	Stops placing text or pictures in the centre.
<font>	Used with other instructions, this code will alter the appearance of your text.
</font>	Stops the change you made to the text.
<font color="red">	Changes all the words that follow to red until </font> stops doing it.
<font size="5">	Makes your text larger or smaller depending upon the number entered, it will stay at that size until </font> is entered.
<img src=" ">	This code will make an image appear on your page (it needs a web address of the picture between the quote marks to work).
<a href=" "> </a>	This pair of codes when used with the address of another web page will create a live clickable link to that web page.

There are a number of other codes which alter the size of pictures and colours; these are used in conjunction with the codes in the table.

HTML codes can be either upper or lower case.

These codes will need to be added to your listings via the HTML 'Details' section when listing your item. There are two tabs: 'Standard' and' HTML'. You may find it easier at first to clear all of the existing code from your page, enter a few codes, and then revert back to the 'standard' view and complete your listing in the traditional way.

Most of the codes I show below work in pairs, a bit like a light switch: one code turns the function on and then a second code will turn it off again. The codes are all contained within angle brackets like these: < and >. The code to turn off a function is a forward slash, like so: /. Therefore, the code to centre an item or picture is <center> and to turn off the function we would use </center>.

Note the American spelling of center!

Background colour

The first thing we shall do is change the background colour of the page. Due to the construction of the eBay listing pages, the code used may seem a little strange if you are familiar with HTML. Try it out and see how you get on.

At the top of your page type this code:

```
<table height="100%" width="100%" bgcolor="Blue">
<tbody>
<tr>
<td>
```

[Your item description and pictures will be placed in this space here.]

```
</td>
</tr>
</tbody>
</table>
```

These few lines will colour your page blue. To make your background yellow, just replace 'blue' with 'yellow' in the code, and so on. (Note that the word color has no letter u; it's the American spelling again. [Ed: I am starting to notice a theme here.])

Outside border

In place of the listing designer offered by eBay, you can create your own border by using some HTML code and save yourself some money on eBay fees. The most basic type of design would just be a single colour border around your description. The code below will create that effect and produce a blue border around a yellow background. To begin with, just delete all the existing code in your description and copy all the following into the page.

```
<center>
<table     height="100%"     cellpadding="15"     width="100%"
bgcolor="blue">
<tbody>
<tr>
<td>
```

```
<table height="100%" width="100%" bgcolor="yellow">

<tbody>

<tr>

<td>

<center>
```

[Your item description and pictures will be placed in this space here.]

```
</center>

</td>

</tr>

</tbody>

</table>

</td>

</tr>

</tbody>

</table>

</center>
```

As before, to change the colour of the border, just replace 'blue' with another colour. To make the border wider, change the number after the word 'cellpadding'; a larger number will make the border wider.

Patterned outside border

To replace the single colour border with a patterned design of your own will require a link to the original image you intend to use. Instead of telling the browser what colour it should be, we will instead refer it to a file stored somewhere on the internet, maybe as a .jpg file on your picture hosting site.

The procedure is much the same as above, but this time the words 'bgcolor=blue' are replaced with background="http://the address of your image.jpg" The code for the template would now read:

```
<center>

<table    height="100%"    cellpadding="15"    width="100%"
background="http:// www.yourname.f2s.com/eBay/photos/car.jpg">

<tbody>
```

```
<tr>
<td>
<table height="100%" width="100%" bgcolor="yellow">
<tbody>
<tr>
<td>
<center>
<p>
```

[Your item description and pictures will be placed in this space here.]

```
</center>
</td>
</tr>
</tbody>
</table>
</td>
</tr>
</tbody>
</table>
</center>
```

By changing the image that you link to, you will be able to create almost any type of border. I have some cute Father Christmas figures during the festive season and a bright yellow sun in the height of summer. I am not really sure if it boosts sales at all but it makes me smile.

Once you have settled on the style of border and colour of background, you can revert back to the standard method of entering your description and the design template you have created will remain and can be used in all of your future listings.

Adding more pictures

If you wish to, you can load more external pictures directly into your description.

We will be using the piece of code that we looked at in the previous section:

```
<img src="http:// the address of your picture is in here.jpg">
```

We can now copy this code directly into the HTML page we have been working on above and this will allow us to add as many pictures as we wish. Your listing design would now look like this:

```
<center>
<table      height="100%"      cellpadding="15"      width="100%"
background="http://thebackgroundimageURL.jpg">
<tbody>
<tr>
<td>
<table height="100%" width="100%" bgcolor="yellow">
<tbody>
<tr>
<td>
<center>
<p>
```
[Your item description will be here and your pictures will appear below.]
```
</center>
<p>
<img src="http://the address of your picture is in here.jpg">
<p>
<img src="http://the address of your picture is in here.jpg">
<p>
<img src="http://the address of your picture is in here.jpg">
<p>
</td>
</tr>
</tbody>
</table>
</td>
```

```
</tr>
</tbody>
</table>
</center>
```

In the above example, I have chosen to load three pictures into the listing, placed them one above the other, separated them with a single line <p>, and centred them on the page by using <center>.

When viewed, your listing will now display the pictures as they were loaded on to your hosting service. If they were not edited before saving to the internet, they could be huge as there is no restriction on the size of these pictures.

Earlier, we looked at the preferred size for a picture, ideally one that would avoid the need for a scroll bar on the screen – a picture size of 640 x 480 pixels would achieve this. You can either edit the pictures before you load them on to your hosting site, or alter the size within your code by using 'height' and 'width' codes. The instruction to load your pictures would then look something like this:

```
<img height="480" width="640" src="http://the address of your picture is in here.jpg">

<p>

<img height="400" width="300" src="http://the address of your picture is in here.jpg">

<p>

<img height="200" width="300" src="http://the address of your picture is in here.jpg">

<p>
```

Each picture would now be a different size; just select the best option for you. The numbers represent how many pixels high and wide your picture is.

 Beware of using the same height and width rules for both landscape and portrait pictures; one or the other will look very strange.

Cross-sell your other listings

We have already looked at some ways of making your visitors aware of your other items. Now we can place direct links to these listings using HTML. The first step is to include a link in the form of a word within a sentence, that when clicked will load your other listings. We can use the same code as before when we were using inserts to link to the eBay home page. To re-cap:

```
<a href="http://eBay.co.uk/">eBay home page</a>
```

This time we will replace the 'eBay.co.uk' with the address of the item we want to link to and change the words 'eBay home page' to describe the auction we are linking to. It could look something like this:

Thanks for visiting our item, please also check out our <a href="http://address of the item you want to show">other great item</a>

If the visitor wants to see the 'other great item', they just click on those words and it will appear.

To get the address of the destination page, you will need to open a second browser window and display the appropriate listing. At the top of the page is the address line; highlight the whole line and copy it. Now paste the line into the sentence above between the quotes. The code will then look something like:

Thanks for visiting our item, please also check out our <a href="http://cgi.eBay.co.uk/ws/eBayISAPI.dll?viewItem&item=601023843592">other great item</a>

(As you can see, it was well worth learning how to copy and paste text, as you don't want to manually type a web address like the one above!)

Practice this process a few times and it should work for you. To link to more than one item, just copy the code and change the address and clickable words.

Adding small pictures to your links

To move things on one stage further, consider the use of a small picture of the item that you wish your visitors to click through to. Not only will you be able to tell them about it, but now they can see it. The HTML code builds on the previous idea and will now include a linked picture of the item as well.

The code will look like this:

Thanks for visiting our item, please also check out our <a href="http://address of the item you want to show"><img src="http://address of the picture.jpg">other great item</a>.

Use the picture that has already been loaded on to eBay for the destination listing. Just locate it again on your Photobucket site or web space, copy its web address and then paste this into the code above.

In summary, to use a picture link to your other listing, you will need both the address of the item and the address of the picture you want to show. Without any further action, the picture of the item on your destination page will appear very large within your description, so we will need to alter the height and width again just as we did when loading in our main pictures. Also, as a default your picture links will have a border; this can be removed by using the code 'border=0'. I will add this below.

If you choose, you could have a key message appear if for any reason your picture fails to load. The example below shows how to add the message "We are always happy to combine lots and reduce postage."

Using HTML, design an email signature that carries a link to your eBay listings or shop. This way, with every email you send, people will receive a small advert for your shop.

Hidden notice boards

It sounds very clever and sophisticated but in fact building a notice board into your eBay description is pretty much the same as loading in an image in the way we have already seen. For most of the time the picture will be the same colour as your background or carry a standard message, the difference is that it can be changed with a few clicks to convey the message of the moment or details of a special offer.

You will need some web space for this to work – sites such as Photobucket are not up to the job. I use the website 50megs but there are dozens out there in cyberspace. The first step is to create a picture, I just use MS Paint because it is easy to use and most PCs have it installed.

This picture is saved to the hosting website and its address is copied into your description, just the same as shown above when we were taking pictures from Photobucket. When you want to show a new message, just create a new picture and replace the original that is saved with the hosting service. The internet address or URL will remain the same but the picture displayed will change. As there is no need to alter the description of your listing – because the web address where it is located remains the same – the new picture will be shown on all listings, past and present.

If you do run into trouble with this, just send me an email (**mollybol@ebaybulletin.co.uk**) and I'll talk you through the process. I may also be able to host your images on my site although please bear in mind that I am not always around so swapping images may take a while.

Full HTML template

A full HTML template including everything we have covered above might end up looking something like the one below.

Sample HTML code for a listing page

<center>

<table   height="100%"   cellpadding="15"   width="100%" background="http://address of your chosen border image.jpg">

<tbody>

<tr>

<td>

<table height="100%" width="100%" bgcolor="yellow">

<tbody>

<tr>

<td>

<center>

<font size="5" color="red">The Title of your Listing </font>

<p>Your description could be written at the top and the pictures displayed below, or swap them around if you so wish.

<p>Use this space to fully describe your item, in this instance it's a selection of Playmobil.

<p>Use text of different <font color="green">colours</font> and <font size="6">sizes</font>.

<p>Convince the visitor that they should bid on or buy your item.

<p>

<center><img src="http://address of your photobucket picture.jpg"

height="480" width="640"></center>

<p>

<center>

Thanks for visiting our listing; please visit us again, we always have new things available.

<p>

Please also check out our <a href="http://address of the listing you want to show"><img height="40" width="50" src="http://address of the picture.jpg" border="0" alt="We are always happy to combine lots & reduce shipping"> Playmobil</a>

and

<a href="http://address of the listing you want to show"> <img height="50" width="40" src="http://address of the picture.jpg" alt="We are always happy to combine lots & reduce shipping">Lego figures</a>.

<p>

</center>

</td>

</tr>

</tbody>

</table>

</td>

</tr>

</tbody>

</table>

</center>

This would appear in your eBay listing as shown in Fig 11.

Fig 11. HTML in use in an item listing

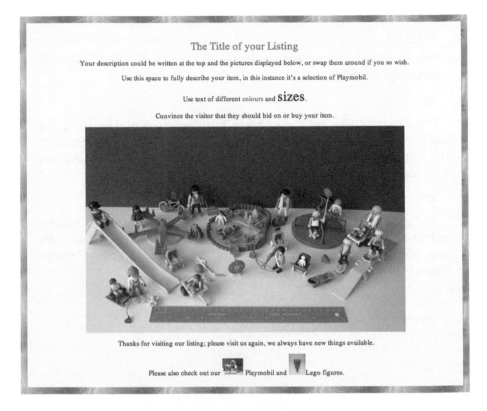

In this example I have chosen a yellow centre space and have changed the size and colour of some words. I have included one picture but to include more just repeat the code. The two small pictures at the bottom of the page are live links; they will take the visitor directly to the listing for the item shown.

The line alt="We are always happy to combine lots & reduce shipping" means this phrase will be shown if there is a problem that means your picture does not load when the customer views the listing.

The great news is that all these additional elements of your listing do not cost any more in fees. By using these techniques in only a handful of listings, you should soon recover the cost of this book in additional sales!

This section has only just touched on the power of HTML to increase the success of your eBay business. There is not enough space to demonstrate all the things you can do, just experiment and you will see that almost anything is possible.

Top five tips for the use of HTML

1. **Don't clutter up your listing**. The more elements you have within your listing, the more baffling it may seem to some buyers – don't get too carried away.

2. **Use moving text and distracting animations only in moderation**. I did not expand on moving text or animations; they can work very well, but could also distract the bidders from their primary objective – to spend money.

3. **Use plain background colours**. Make your listing easy to read. Simple, bright colours work best for my market of toys and cosmetics. If you are selling Warhammer or gothic-themed items then a darker more striking design could be the way to go.

4. **Make use of external links**. They remove the clutter and allow you to add value to your description in many ways.

5. **Use large pictures within the description**. Large pictures sell items.

Summary

You should now:

- Be proficient in the basic computer techniques of copying and pasting and opening multiple browser windows.
- Understand how to use inserts, including creating links to external web pages and pictures.
- Know how to include extra pictures in your item listing.
- Know how to use basic HTML to enhance the look of your eBay pages.

You've come a long way! You now know how to list items on eBay and how to make your item pages attractive and sophisticated, such that they will be better than 95% of the competition. However, don't get too confident just yet. There's an important chapter coming up next – on fraud!

EIGHT

FRAUD ON EBAY

Overview

In any environment where money changes hands there is the potential for fraud. eBay is no exception to this rule. There is fraud on the site and it can be costly if you are affected. Knowing what to look for and applying a little caution in your eBay dealings should significantly limit your chances of becoming a victim.

There is an old saying that if something seems too good to be true, then it probably is. This is as true on eBay as anywhere. Beware of the listing that claims to have a genuine article for sale at one-tenth of the retail price – you may well end up with something not quite as you expected.

There are several areas of potential fraud within eBay: sellers may try to relieve you of your money under false pretences, buyers can purchase items and then default on payment, and your eBay or PayPal accounts can be broken into.

This chapter will look at some of the fraudulent techniques that I am aware of, along with a few examples of what to look out for. It is by no means a comprehensive list as the fraudsters are coming up with new scams all the time.

The items I sell have an average sale price of just £10, so my experience of being defrauded by buyers is limited. If I were to sell higher-value items, I am sure that it would increase.

Just how big a target you will be as a seller on eBay will be decided by the kind of items you sell and their value. High value negotiable items, such as mobile phones or computers, are more likely to be a target than your cherished Val Doonican LPs.

Types of fraud

The areas of potential fraud we will look at are:

1. Payment fraud.

2. Postage fraud.

3. eBay account hijack.

4. PayPal account hijack.

These are explained below.

1. Payment fraud

Receiving payment for an item is great and is the reward for all your hard work. However, there is always a concern that the payment may not be good; perhaps the cheque will bounce or the electronic payment may be retracted. This is more of a concern for international sales and for items with a high value.

The majority of payments will be fine and there are a few simple precautions to follow to help ensure a trouble-free completion to your trade.

1. Do not sell your item outside of the eBay process. It is possible to end an auction early and sell to the highest bidder, or place a new Buy It Now listing for a pre-determined price. Selling items outside of the process, though, will remove any seller protection that may apply and of course you will not be eligible for feedback. Some buyers will offer you this option and angle for a price reduction in the knowledge that you will save on eBay fees; a 10% saving can be tempting but I would advise against this.

2. Check the winning buyer's details. Are you happy with their feedback comments, if they have any? Check the member's contact information against the postal address provided by the buyer. If anything does not appear to be correct, don't send the item and contact eBay with your concerns.

3. Is the trade covered by any fraud or seller protection? If the payment has been received electronically, check the service being used and see if the trade is covered by a protection policy. If there is such a policy, ensure that you comply with the terms of this cover. The most common problem that I am aware of is where the buyer asks for the item to be shipped to a different address, possibly in a different country. This will be more of a concern for higher priced or popular items.

 A buyer in the UK made a purchase from me and then asked for it to be sent into the 'Gazza strip' [sic]. As this was a first for me I held off for a day or two and sure enough the payment had been made with a stolen PayPal account. No harm done this time, but it does pay to be vigilant.

4. Ensure that payment clears before sending the item. Standard cheques can be presented to your bank and eCheques work in the same way: after a few days they are cleared. If the buyer is paying with a credit card, you can contact the credit card company if in any doubt and confirm the identity of the buyer.

I choose not to accept credit cards directly, only via PayPal.

Use good judgement when accepting a cheque or money order as payment for a high-value item. Before posting the item, check with your bank to ensure that the payment method is valid and that funds have cleared and are available. If you have reason to believe that the buyer paid, or is attempting to pay, with fraudulent funds, contact eBay so that they can investigate and take appropriate action.

 I have had only two bounced cheques so far, both for small amounts where unfortunately I had already dispatched the items. eCheques often fail to clear but as I don't dispatch until they do it is annoying but not costly.

In the event that the buyer sends payment that is found to be fraudulent, contact the police in your area and the area where the buyer resides. eBay will fully cooperate with all such inquiries. If payment is reversed, stopped, or cannot be received, you should also contact the payment issuer (credit card company, issuing bank, PayPal, etc.) to review the options available to you.

If you have already sent the item and have been unable to receive payment, review the 'Defrauded Sellers' page on eBay for other options you can pursue.

If you are unable to receive payment, you may also be able to request a final value fee credit by filing a claim under the unpaid item process.

Five areas of extra caution for a seller

1. **International payment**. International payments are likely to be received via PayPal or similar companies and could also include eCheques (eChecks). Let these run their course before dispatching. If you do take any overseas personal cheques, remember that they take a lot longer to clear.

2. **Revised shipping information**. If you are asked to ship your item to an address other than a verified one shown on the PayPal documentation be wary and check a bit deeper.

3. **Unknown or new buyers**. New bidders will not have a track record with eBay. If selling a high-value item check their contact information and maybe even give them a call before sending the item.

4. **Unusual bidding activity**. If your auction item reaches a level that you didn't expect you are either very lucky or there may be a problem when the auction ends. Check the bidding history of the two highest bidders using the advanced search and see if they have been active in the same auctions before. If in any doubt, ask for more information from them.

5. **Orders shipped 'rush' or overnight**. Be cautious if you are asked to ship the item in a hurry; a birthday is the most popular excuse given when this is requested.

2. Postage fraud

eBay encourages buyers and sellers to resolve any issues involving shipping by communicating directly with each other. If you have a specific question about shipping and handling charges, refer to the eBay help pages on selling practices for information: pages.ebay.co.uk/help/policies/selling-practices.html

If an item was lost or damaged in the post, you can request contact information from eBay and call your trading partner to explain the situation and work out a solution. You should also consider contacting the postal service for assistance. If you send a notification of shipment when you dispatch the item, your buyer will be expecting it and should contact you if it doesn't arrive in a reasonable time. This will happen in one of two ways: they will either send you an email, which is fine, or open a dispute case, which is not so good.

It is very difficult to prove if an item did arrive and the buyer is just claiming that it didn't – especially if the buyer is overseas. For higher-value items, incorporate an insurance cost into the postage charge and use an alternative postal service that will be tracked.

Items that are lost or damaged in the post are covered under the buyer protection programme. The process to use is accessed via the 'Resolution Centre' (go to Help > Resolution Centre) or use the shortcut towards the bottom of your My eBay page.

If you have paid for an item but didn't receive it, or you paid for and received an item, but it was significantly different from the item description, e.g. broken, then you will be covered. All you have to do is contact eBay via the Resolution Centre, there are links to this at various places throughout eBay. It is worth noting that eBay can only refund your payment if you used PayPal.

- eBay will review the information provided and get back to you within 48 hours.

- If you haven't received your item they will refund you (including original postage costs), using PayPal.

- If your item was not as described, eBay will help you with the returns process and then refund you using PayPal.

 If you register your complaint with PayPal instead of eBay, you'll be taken automatically to PayPal to file a PayPal Buyer Protection claim.

Over the past few years the number of items reported missing en route has risen to a ridiculous level. They cannot just be lost down the back of a filing cabinet, somebody is stealing them. It might be somebody within the postal system or it could be your buyer.

For items over £30 in value or when multiple items creep over £30 I will use the recorded delivery service (current cost £1.10) and absorb the extra expense. If the item is particularly big or weighs more than 2 kilos then I will use myHermes, who include insurance up to £50 for free and, unlike the Royal Mail, myHermes will actually pay up if a parcel is lost. I do tell my customers that items over £30 could be sent this way – a great example of using HTML via your noticeboards to inform your customers of policy changes.

If an item is lost somewhere in the system and you have to refund the buyer be sure to add the person to your blocked bidder list – you can find this towards the bottom of your My eBay page. If they did steal the item then you certainly don't want to trade with them again; if there was a problem within the delivery network then you don't want to send anything else into the same black hole.

As you would expect after such a long time on eBay my 'blocked bidder list' has grown into quite a beast. If you would like a copy of my list please just send me an email; you can then paste it into your own list with ease.

Five things to make sure of when shipping

1. **Obtain a certificate of posting**. It is free and will help if you need to claim for a lost item. The proof of postage will of course also show that you did send the item.

2. **Insure high-value items**. This will add a relatively small amount in costs in comparison to the value of the item. If offering the free postage option build the cost into the asking price and mention in your description how you will dispatch.

3. **Wait for payment to clear**. It is such an important point that it needs to be mentioned again: especially with higher-value items, only ship when the money is safely tucked up in your account.

4. **Include a return address**. Add a return address on the back of each parcel; there is always a chance that it might find its way back to you.

5. **Advise the buyer when the item is sent**. As soon as you dispatch the item, click the little parcel icon next to your item details in My eBay and the system will send a dispatch notification – well they should, although I suspect sometimes they don't always get sent. It is great for customer care and will give your customer an idea of when they can expect delivery.

3. eBay account hijack

One of the most popular pastimes of fraudsters is trying to gain access to your eBay account. They will do this by sending spoof emails to you in many different formats, each designed to have you enter your eBay ID and password on to a website that you accessed via the email.

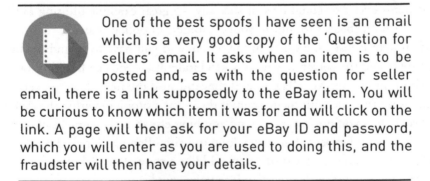 One of the best spoofs I have seen is an email which is a very good copy of the 'Question for sellers' email. It asks when an item is to be posted and, as with the question for seller email, there is a link supposedly to the eBay item. You will be curious to know which item it was for and will click on the link. A page will then ask for your eBay ID and password, which you will enter as you are used to doing this, and the fraudster will then have your details.

These emails, also referred to as 'phishing' emails, could claim that you have been invited to become a PowerSeller, or that your account details are incorrect. They may warn you that if you do not verify your details immediately your account will be suspended. The list of inventive excuses is growing longer every week.

For a heads up on the latest spoofs and phishing emails be sure to sign up for my weekly bulletin. Readers who spot something untoward email the details to me and I publish for all to see.

All of these deceptions have one goal: to take temporary control of your eBay account.

Once fraudsters have control, your password will be changed, locking you out of your own account. While eBay investigate the situation, a number of things will happen. Firstly, the account ID into which you receive electronic payments (this is usually your email address) will be changed. A number of high-value items will be listed under your account; these will be very popular items offered with a Buy It Now option well below the average price for the item. They will stipulate that only electronic payment can be used to buy them.

Any potential bargain hunters will find the items; they may even check your feedback, which will be very good and they may decide to purchase. When they pay, the money will be transferred to a different account and of course no item will be dispatched. You have been used to exploit the buyer, who will lose their money.

The best advice I can give is to never click on a link contained in an email. If the note is from eBay, it will appear in your messages folder found on your My eBay page.

Generally, all purchases by eligible buyers that meet policy conditions and that do not fall within an exclusion or coverage limitation are covered by eBay's Money Back Guarantee. For full details of the buyer protection programme check the main help page:

pages.ebay.co.uk/help/policies/money-back-guarantee.html

Protect your eBay identity

Now would be a great time to revisit your security measures just to be on the safe side. These are my recommendations for a secure password and restful nights:

- Ensure your password is longer than four characters in length because there are a number of programs available commercially that can instantly hack a password of four characters or less (eBay recommend at least six characters).

- Use a mixture of upper and lower case letters; this is an aspect of the PayPal password security (for some reason eBay treat upper and lower case in the same way). Adding an upper case letter adds to the complexity, but is not enough on its own.

- Include numbers and ASCII characters; an ASCII character is basically anything that appears on your keyboard such as !â?Â£$%^&*()>?:@{}. Add these into your password along with a number or two and the time taken to crack your password is significantly increased.

- Use a word that doesn't exist; have you ever suffered a dictionary attack? Some password hacking programs run through every word in the dictionary until they find your password. The more logical the word, the easier it is to find it. Even joining two words together doesn't slow them down very much.

So an ideal password is one that is a mixture of upper and lower case, is longer than 4 characters, includes numbers and ASCII symbols and is not a real word – that should be easy to remember then!

eBay will block sellers who are trying to list from a computer they don't normally use. If you're listing from a different computer (e.g. at a friend's house, at the library), you will be asked for some additional verification to make sure it's really you listing the item.

To help with this process you should:

- Check that your personal information is current. eBay might need to confirm the information on your account, such as your telephone number or address. You should provide a secondary phone number (for example a mobile number for when you are on the go).

- Review your secret question. Make sure the secret question and answer you have on file is easy for you to remember and difficult for others to guess. I write all my passwords on a piece of paper and leave it with my front door key under a flower pot – security is priority number one at Molly HQ.

Just time for a quick word of warning to all business sellers out there. If you are a business you are required to have your address on every listing. This could prove a problem should your holiday settings be on as thieves may conclude that you are away and that all your stock is still indoors. Consider using a different address for correspondence which should make it a little harder to work out where the stock is.

If you do find that your eBay account has been compromised get in touch with eBay Live help, who should be able to assist:

ocsnext.ebay.co.uk/ocs/cuhome?ref=1

4. PayPal account hijack

A similar process is used to try and gain control of your PayPal account. Many emails are sent asking you to verify your PayPal details, or warning you that an unauthorised change has been made.

Once the fraudster has an account, they will bid in pairs on an eBay item, usually high-end such as a mobile phone. The bidding will be raised much higher than the value of the item to ensure they win it. When the auction ends, payment will be made and you will be asked to send the item to a different address than that shown on the PayPal documentation. Having achieved a much higher price than you expected, you may well agree and post the item once the funds have been received in your account.

A stolen PayPal account can be used in the same way to purchase an item outright, so if you have fixed-price or shop listings, beware.

When the PayPal account is restored back to its correct owner, the payment will be recovered from the seller and placed back in the PayPal account – this is known as a chargeback – leaving the seller with no money and no item.

What eBay will and won't do concerning fraud

eBay have an interest in making the site as free from fraud as possible, as the threat of being defrauded will deter some people from trading. The scale of the site makes policing every trade impossible; there is just too much happening at any one time.

eBay provides the venue for buyers and sellers to come together and trade. They can take action against members who break the rules, but they do rely on the wider community to report such activity.

What eBay does

When suspicious activity is reported to eBay, they will investigate the circumstances and then either warn or suspend members that are found to violate eBay policies.

eBay provide the framework and systems that allow buyers and sellers to obtain contact information from each other. Before a trade is completed, it is possible to find out a considerable amount of information about a member and following the completion of a trade more personal information is made available.

eBay works closely with PayPal to help buyers and sellers resolve transaction problems. For items paid for with PayPal, buyers may file a complaint through the PayPal Buyer Protection process. For all other items, eBay provide the 'item not received' or 'item not as described' process.

The vast majority of eBay buyers receive their items quickly and smoothly. However, if you don't receive your item or if it arrives and is not as described, then you can receive the full value of your purchase (including postage) back when you have paid with PayPal.

PayPal protection eligibility requirements are as follows:

- Claims must be made for tangible, non-prohibited goods that can be posted.

- The "This item is fully protected when you pay with PayPal" message is displayed in the seller listing information.

- Buyers must raise a dispute within 45 days (soon to be 180 days) of a single PayPal payment for the full price of the item. If no satisfactory response is received from the seller, a claim must be escalated within 20 days of raising the dispute.

- The payment must have been made using the 'Pay now' button on eBay or by associating the payment with the eBay item number on the PayPal site. You must use the seller's email address associated with the listing.

- Buyers cannot make multiple claims on the same payment.

What eBay does not do

eBay is unable to take action on a member's behalf. This includes contacting a member directly to ask about the status of an item. They will provide contact information, but will not become directly involved in the dispute.

Since eBay is not involved in the actual transaction, they cannot force a member to live up to their obligation. This also includes pursuing any action outside of the eBay community, which will be up to the individual member to follow.

What to do if you have been defrauded

eBay urges buyers and sellers to use both email and the telephone to contact one another to resolve any issues that may arise. You can get the phone number for your trading partner by going to 'Find contact information' under 'Advanced search'. Most issues can be resolved through direct communication between buyers and sellers; quite often it is just a misunderstanding.

If efforts to communicate directly with your buyer or seller are unsuccessful, consider the following:

• Contact PayPal if this method of payment was used. You may be covered by PayPal Buyer Protection.

• If you did not pay through PayPal, contact your credit card company or payment issuer. Credit card issuers typically provide protection in instances of online fraud. Your credit card company will be able to tell you what type of coverage they provide.

• Use eBay's Resolution Centre. Through this dispute process, trading partners are able to communicate online to resolve transaction problems. If problems cannot be resolved, buyers may then submit an eBay Standard Purchase Protection claim. eBay also reviews disputes for possible violations of the seller non-performance policy.

• Contact the police. To find the contact details for your local police force go to: www.police.uk/forces.htm

Summary

You should now:

• Understand the types of fraud that exist on eBay.

• Know what eBay will and will not do.

• Know what to do if you've been the subject of fraud.

Not a pleasant topic, fraud, but it has to be dealt with. A more attractive topic is covered in the next chapter – how to develop your business and make more money.

NINE

DEVELOPING YOUR EBAY BUSINESS

Overview

As your experience of eBay grows, along with your ability to manage all aspects of your business, you may decide to move up to the next level. This may involve dedicating more time to your enterprise, which should result in more rewards. eBay is completely flexible: if you are content with a certain income and workload, remain at that level; if, on the other hand, you would like to develop your business, there are a few approaches which can be considered.

I started my eBay adventure way back in January 2002; looking back to how I first operated it was a very small undertaking, but even then I knew it could be something more if I wanted it to be.

As nobody in my family had a business which I could adapt I drifted into selling something that I knew a lot about – toys. With three kids I had a good knowledge of which toys held their value and also held together after hours of play. To find these I went to car boot sales, in fact I still do. Toys still form a good part of my turnover, too, particularly at Christmas.

As all of my beloved children are girls I soon amassed an unhealthy knowledge of cosmetics and skin care; I probably know more about lipsticks and mascara than any man should. Armed with this expertise I branched out into cosmetics. This has become my mainstay product line and I launched it as a limited company in June 2013.

My love of property and keen eye soon resulted in a more masculine pastime – the sale of DIY accessories. This is a more recent business undertaking but has already outstripped toys to be my second placed activity by turnover.

As for the future, who knows, I just keep my eyes and mind open.

The ideas that I will mention here are my thoughts on a possible way forward. How you actually grow your enterprise will depend on many things, but I hope I stimulate a few ideas.

Building on your brand

Now you have successfully traded on eBay, even just once, you have the beginnings of a brand – a name that customers will associate with certain levels of service and product quality. If the buying experience was a good one, your customers may well return to see if you have other items of interest. It is possible to use this goodwill to drive as many visits to your listings as possible.

This section looks at some of the options that will help to build your business reputation and gives some ideas on how to encourage customers to return. The ultimate goal must be to ensure that each time the individual visits eBay, they will visit your listings or eBay shop.

eBay shops

Opening an eBay shop could be the next step for your online business. Shop inventory items operate in much the same way as ordinary fixed-price listings, but there are quite a few advantages, especially if you are selling the same item again and again.

All the shops on eBay can be browsed, in just the same way as you would by visiting a traditional shopping mall. Shops are listed in a directory in the same way that the main categories are structured, so you can browse through similar shops if you are looking for a particular item.

eBay have created a number of tools specifically for the shop owner. These will enable you to develop your eBay brand and should encourage buyers to buy more products.

These management tools include:

- Customisation – have complete control over the look and feel of your shop (colours, graphics, content, etc.).

- Organise and display your items with your own custom categories.

- Keyword searches within your shop, which buyers can use to find goods.

- Control the cross-promotion of your other items when buyers view, bid on, or buy an item.

- A unique internet web address (URL) that you can promote to your buyers. This address will appear on external search engines – Google, Bing, Yahoo, etc. – driving potential customers directly to your shop.

- Sales and visitor traffic reports to let you know how successful your shop is.

Three formats of eBay shop

There are three formats for an eBay shop:

1. Basic.

2. Featured.

3. Anchor.

There are some criteria to meet before you can open a shop, which vary according to the type of shop. Currently the criteria are:

Basic shop:

- You must have a minimum feedback score of 10, or

- You must be PayPal verified.

Featured shop:

- You must be a registered business seller on eBay.

- You must be PayPal verified.

- Maintain a 12-month average detailed seller ratings score of 4.4 or above in each of the four detailed seller rating areas.

Anchor shop:

- You must be a registered business seller on eBay.

- You must be PayPal verified.

- You must maintain a 12-month average detailed seller ratings score of 4.6 or above in each of the four areas (see p. 25 for a list of the four areas).

The three types of shop are explained in more detail below.

Basic shop

A Basic shop subscription includes the following:

- Ability to create a customised, professional-looking shop quickly.

- Advanced merchandising and cross-promotion tools.

- Sales Reports Plus to track and evaluate your eBay sales activity.

- Real-time shop traffic reports, including page views, referring web addresses and keywords used by potential buyers (available only on eBay.co.uk).

- Inclusion in the eBay shop directory (stores.eBay.co.uk).

- Automatic optimisation of your shop pages to obtain the best possible rankings on search engines.

- Five additional customisable shop pages.

Featured shop

With a Featured shop, you get all the Basic shop benefits, plus:

- eBay Selling Manager Pro for free!

- Advanced shop traffic reporting (eBay.co.uk only).

- Sales Reports Plus with marketplace data.

- Ten additional customisable shop pages.

Anchor shop

With an Anchor shop, you get all the Basic and Featured shop benefits, plus 15 additional customisable shop pages.

The Mollybol Shop

Ok, so it is not the best shop name in the world as it does not really describe what is on offer; however, due to the unusual nature of my day-to-day activities, and appearances in the media, Mollybol has become my brand and people do search for it.

I now have three eBay shops and all are currently Basic; this means that I pay a flat fee each month and this allows listings to be placed at a cost of 10p each. (We covered fees a little earlier in this book but I will re-cap below.) The other benefits of a shop apply, but the main thing for me is that I can list an item and leave it in the shop for a whole year at a cost of just £1.20.

I have chosen a standard shop layout as it is the format most buyers have become used to; the only real difference is a little HTML down the left side to promote my books.

Drop by any time: stores.ebay.co.uk/The-Mollybol-Shop

Shop categories

Assigning your inventory a category within your shop is in my opinion a must as it makes related items much easier to find. This is addressed during the listing process just after you select the main eBay category. Three levels of shop category are allowed, for example: 'Toys' could be the main category, 'Lego' a sub-category of 'Toys', and then 'Wheels' as a sub-category of 'Lego'. Why not take a look at my shop and see how it works for the cosmetics side of things.

Categories can come and go and one will only appear in your shop if it has an item listed within it. The catch-all category is 'Other'; avoid dumping your items in this as it can be hard to wade through. Special categories for 'Stocking fillers', 'Sale items', 'Weird & wonderful' can be created and used seasonally.

I can create up to 300 categories, which is ample; searching through 50 is hard enough. I tend to place my most popular main category at the top of the list and then list subcategories in alphabetical order.

One final note on category structure: opt to display all category levels on your shop home page and show your buyer what is on offer.

Although you should select the correct eBay category for your item, within your shop you can insert an item where you wish. Place similar items together even if they are not technically the same. My 'Tomy' Trains sit in my 'Thomas the Tank Engine' category as a buyer may be interested in both.

If a category grows too big and needs to be split into two subcategories, don't amend your items one by one. Instead create your new categories and use the 'Edit listings in bulk' facility, as shop categories are one of the options that can be changed with this tool.

Shop management

Thankfully you will probably only have to set up your shop once and then maybe tinker with it over time. Once you subscribe to an eBay shop a section within your My eBay called Manage my Shop will appear, and spookily this is where we are going next.

Down the left side of the page are a number of shop design options, and categories we have covered. The other two main areas are Display settings and Promotion boxes.

Display settings

Here you can name your shop, write a brief description of what you are about, select a shop theme and choose from a list of shop options.

I have opted for a gallery view arranged by 'Newly listed'; I am a picture kind of guy and feel that images will attract interest. The other option is to show your items in a list. It is all down to personal choice.

Promotion boxes

I use four promotion boxes, two at the top of the shop page and two down the left side. The top two show the most recently listed items and those ending soonest. The other two, which appear under the shop categories, I use to promote my books and encourage signatures for my shop newsletters. If you select 'Custom' you can input any HTML or text you wish, including pictures and links. See the HTML chapter earlier in this book for a few ideas.

Marketing tools

eBay also offer the shop owner a range of tools to help with the day-to-day running. As with all marketing aids, some work well and some don't work at all. Here are a few worth checking out:

Listing frame

This option allows you to decide how your listings will be seen by customers. This key information will appear just above the description in your listings. There are a number of options, just click what you want to include.

As I still don't have a shop logo, my listing frame includes:

- My shop name.
- Five category tabs, which when clicked display all items in that shop category. I change these to promote new lines.
- A shop search box.
- A link that allows buyers to sign up for my newsletters.
- A link to my items on sale.
- A personal marketing message that recognises the visitor and directs them into my shop.

Markdown manager

This facility does just what it says, allowing the shop owner to reduce the price of items – thus creating a sale.

You just need to select which items you want to reduce, when you want to start the sale and how much you want to reduce by. A sale can last up to 14 days; however, due to current restrictions some listings cannot be put on sale if they are newly listed, or if the price has recently changed.

Sales are great – for most things – but I would be a little cautious about running a sale on perishable items such as cosmetics as the inference could be that the items are close to their use by date and need to be shifted.

I will often run 24 or 48 hour sales to increase cash flow and keep my army of Elves employed; too much tea and cake with their feet up is bad for them.

Shop holiday settings

If you have an eBay shop and decide to take a well-earned break you can shut your shop and hide all fixed-price listings without having to remove them from the site. Holiday settings can be found in My eBay and have three main options:

1. Hide and block purchases for my fixed price listings. Note: This doesn't affect your auction-style listings.

2. Display a return date. This is straightforward, just select the date you will be back. Selecting both should result in no sales and no adverse feedback for slow delivery if you were away on holiday. I say should, but sometimes those dear customers find a way. During my two week break in 2009 I averaged six sales per day even though I had implemented all the 'I am shut' options.

3. To address the possibility of disgruntled customers and poor feedback add a note to your automatic emails outlining how long it will be before you can post; at least your buyer will be aware. Turn on your 'Out of office email' response and compose an appropriate message. If you decided to use HTML within your listing and included a hidden notice board, use this to inform anybody who finds your listings that you are away from the office.

If I am away for more than a couple of days I will shut down all shops and block anybody from making a purchase. Two days before I am due to return I will remove the block on fixed-price item purchase, now buyers can shop but a message will still be displayed saying that there will be a delay in dispatch. The night before I return I will turn off all holiday settings as I am likely to meet my one day dispatch goal upon my return.

One thing I have noticed is that when your full holiday settings are on and you decide to make fixed-price listings available you cannot just 'unclick' the 'hide and block' box, it doesn't seem to work. Instead you need to remove all holiday settings and then activate them again, but this time leave that box unchecked – what a pain.

Shop fees

To open an eBay shop you pay a monthly subscription fee. Within this price are included a number of free listings, so if you have a basic shop and 200 listings then you have maximised the deal. Each item you list in your eBay shop incurs an insertion fee and, if it sells, a final value fee. The subscription fees and insertion fees are as shown in Table 15. Table 16 shows the Basic shop fees for private sellers.

Table 15. Shop fees (business sellers)

			Insertion fees			
Your approx. listings per month	Shop level	Monthly subscription	Free fixed-price listings	Price per additional fixed-price listing	Price per auction starting under £1	Price per auction starting at £1 or more
Up to 65	None	Free	0	£0.30	£0.10	£0.30
65–600	Basic	£19.99	200	£0.10	£0.05	£0.15
600–5000	Featured	£59.99	1200	£0.05	£0.05	£0.15
Over 5000	Anchor	£249.99	Unlimited	Free	£0.05	£0.15

Note: You may be subject to selling limits if, for example, you've fallen below standard or you're a new seller.

Table 16. Basic shop fees (private sellers)

Monthly cost	What's included
£19.99	100 free auction-style or fixed-price listings per month. After that they're £0.35 each.
	Free scheduler for 100 listings per month. After that they're £0.06 each.
	8% final value fees. You'll never pay more than £75 per item.

Shops also have the option to place listings that are 'Good 'til cancelled', these are recurring 30-day listings. eBay will charge the relevant fees every 30 days. Watch out if you go for the subtitle or similar cost upgrade, as when the listing rolls over to the next month you will be charged again for this upgrade.

Note: Shop insertion fees covers any quantity of items per listing.

If you list more than 65 fixed-price BIN items per month, it may be cost effective to open a Basic shop as the lower insertion fees should make the overall costs lower.

eBay shops are certainly well suited for sellers who stock repeat items. The 'Good 'til cancelled' option means that one listing can run for months, significantly reducing admin time. Sellers with large numbers of items for sale at any one time can also make good use of shops as they have the facility for buyers to perform keyword searches within the shop.

Recent changes to the pricing structure have seen many specialist shops selling books, stamps and records close. These items are listed one at a time; they cannot take advantage of the multiple item discounts or benefit from higher search positioning resulting from high sales from a single listing.

Seller tools

It is in eBay's interest for sellers to be able to manage more listings and sell more products; they will, of course, make more money from our fees. To assist the seller with some of the less interesting tasks, eBay has developed a number of seller tools. There will undoubtedly be more tools released in the coming years but at this time there are three tools which might be of interest to you and these are worthy of a little more detail:

1. Selling Manager.
2. Selling Manager Pro.
3. Turbo Lister.

These are explained below.

1. Selling Manager

Selling Manager is a management tool that will assist with a wide range of tasks, from scheduling your listings to managing your sales; it even helps print address labels. This tool will work within your My eBay section and is compatible with all other eBay tools, such as the standard 'Sell an item' form which we looked at earlier.

Selling Manager will provide an immediate estimate of your total sales and switch back to the original My eBay format at any time. This service is currently free of charge although you do have to subscribe; just visit the Seller Tool Finder from the Site Map and upgrade online.

The features offered by Selling Manager are as follows:

- View the status of your listings and reminders of what to do next in the Summary view.

- Manage items to be listed at a future date using Scheduled view.

- Track your active listings using Active view.

- Manage the items that you have sold using Sold view.

- Re-list items from your Unsold view.

- Track and manage post-sales activities including feedback, email, payments and dispatch.
- Accomplish tasks in bulk including listing items, re-listing your unsold items, leaving feedback, sending email and printing invoices.
- Download your sales records.

2. Selling Manager Pro

As you have come to expect, eBay like to relieve you of as much wonga as possible and so offer an upgrade to the Selling Manager service – Selling Manager Pro. This service costs £4.99 per month. This tool is free if you opt for a Featured shop.

This tool has been created for the high-volume seller and small business. It will allow for bulk listings and builds on the Selling Manager management tools. The additional facilities include:

- Inventory management. Manage your auctions and shop items by keeping track of your inventory. It is not good to have stock in storage that you don't know about. It is also not good to sell an item and then realise that you don't have any left. You can also re-list your items in bulk.
- Listing statistics. Understand the success of your product and see which items sell best by calculating your average selling price.
- Listing, emailing, sending feedback and printing invoices in bulk. Selling Manager Pro will perform most of your mundane tasks in bulk.
- Automatic completion of feedback and email generation.
- Profit and loss reports. With monthly profit and loss reports, you will be able to stay better informed about how your business and the market in general is performing. These reports include your eBay fees.

I am a big fan of Selling Manager Pro, it could even be the best £4.99 I spend each month. The automatic feedback saves me hours of tedious admin, leaving more time for coffee.

I have set the automatic system to leave feedback when my buyer has paid and left me a positive rating. This approach may reduce my feedback score – as some people won't leave feedback until they get it from me – but I still can't bring myself to leave feedback on receipt of payment.

The small fee to schedule a listing in advance is removed when you subscribe to Selling Manager Pro, so if you schedule enough items it could be worth it for that alone.

3. Turbo Lister

Listing can be very time consuming, especially if you have to write out the description each time. eBay have thought of this and produced a tool called Turbo Lister. As the name suggests, this is a very fast way of loading hundreds or even thousands of items on to eBay in one go.

With this tool, you will be able to create your listings on your computer and then upload them to eBay in one hit. It has been designed for medium to high-volume sellers and is currently free to use. Some of the main attractions of Turbo Lister are:

- It contains a design editor which will help create a more professional listing and you don't need to know any HTML.

- You can load multiple items once and save the details for use in the future, which saves writing them out again.

- You can add pictures to the listings without being connected to the internet.

- You can insert notes on payment terms, shipping details and any other messages that you would normally include.

 As Turbo Lister is free, try it and see how you get on. Some sellers – myself included – just don't like it, but you won't know unless you try.

Seller tool fees

Table 17. eBay Seller tool fees

Listing tool	Fee
Selling Manager	Free
Selling Manager Pro	£4.99 per month
Turbo Lister	Free

Encourage repeat sales

Once established, you will attract repeat visits as regular customers check back to see what you have for sale. Increasing and maintaining this customer loyalty will result in more sales and ultimately higher profits. To give some kind of appreciation of this, my cosmetic shop sees around 11% repeat customers each month. A satisfied customer who returns several times is also more likely to be lenient and understanding if a problem does occur, such as sending the wrong item. This is quite a frequent occurrence at HQ as so many lipsticks look the same and the writing on them is very small. Don't even get me started on mascaras!

There are several things that can be done to increase this customer return rate – they are all based around the customer experience.

- Hold items. Be prepared to hold items while customers continue to shop with you. Offer a discount on postage for multiple purchases or maybe a free mini mascara (or whatever it is you sell) if they buy three items.

- List regularly. Remain well stocked with items. Customers may return a couple of times, but if they do not see any items for sale, they may not return again.

- Sell similar items over a number of days. If you are selling a collection of items by auction, list them over a number of days. Mention that you will have more of the same tomorrow and bidders will return each day to see what is new. Make sure that you cross-sell other items that might also be of interest.

- Specialise. If you specialise in one particular line, you will establish a regular customer base. If ever they need that certain item, they will visit you to see what is available. Use additional IDs for different types of item. This is precisely why I split the DIY away from the cosmetics, as although I have sold many thermostatic radiator valves to ladies the demand for nail varnish from builders was limited to say the least.

Create a USP for your business

A Unique Selling Point, or USP, is just a smart way of saying that you need to differentiate your business from the competition. Go one step further in some areas and stand out from the crowd. Buyers will visit you again because of that little extra you offer; they may also mention it in their feedback comment, which can only help.

Here are some ideas for how you can go one better than the competition:
- Speed of dispatch. Quick dispatch of items will certainly improve your repeat business. Once an item has been bought and paid for, the buyer wants it the

very next day. Don't promise what cannot be delivered, but send items as quick as you can. This also gets them out of the way and saves on storage space.

- Returns policy. Work within the eBay rules and develop a simple, no quibble, returns policy. Be wary though of the customer who buys to try and then returns. Experience will show the best returns policy for your line of business. If somebody can buy knowing that the item can be returned under certain circumstances, they will have more confidence in you as a seller.

- Customer service. Use the eBay system to send an acknowledgement email following purchase, payment and again on dispatch of goods. Include a note in each parcel to close the trade and invite the buyer back.

- Quality of packing. This has been mentioned many times already, but it is one of the big areas where you can impress your buyer. Good packing will entice them to return to you, knowing that great care will be taken with their items. I use nice clean packing materials when sending cosmetics and all my recycled materials when sending central heating pumps or shower spares.

- Free samples. This is a sales ploy that I have used to great advantage to generate more sales and maybe even a little loyalty.

 When you have decided on your key areas, write them in your item listings; tell your customers what you will do, above and beyond what they might expect.

I have settled on three areas of my business where I try to excel. I aim to achieve them with every trade, they are:

1. Quality of packing.

2. Speed of dispatch.

3. Communications throughout the transaction.

Once you have established your operating processes, it will become second nature to pack in a certain way, or send emails at certain stages of the trade. My feedback comments from customers are full of references to these three areas – it really works.

Why feedback is so important

Feedback is perhaps the main reason that eBay has become so successful. Without it, how would you know that the seller will do what they say? On the strength of a feedback score, we will send money to a complete stranger – possibly in a different country – in the hope and expectation that they will send us some goods. It is very powerful!

Maintaining a 100% feedback score as a seller is very difficult. It is extremely hard to please everybody all of the time and negative feedbacks will happen; it is only to be expected if you have been trading for some time.

Sellers can only leave positive feedback for buyers and that positive rating cannot contain any negative comments. This is not one of eBay's best ideas in my humble opinion; in fact it is the subject of quite a few emails to the eBay bulletin – not many sellers like it!

Feedback as a sales tool

We have already discussed how positive feedback can be obtained by really pleasing your customer and this will work in your favour to stimulate further sales. How you leave your feedback for buyers may also influence your sales. In the first place, I suggest that you always leave feedback for your buyers. I only leave feedback if a positive comes my way first, but you may not want to follow my lead on this. For many new members, feedback is vital and if they suspect that you may not leave feedback, they may be deterred from trading with you. How you actually leave feedback is also something to be considered. Choose the words you use so that the buyer feels special; it may just prompt them to buy from you again in the future.

Coping with negative feedback

Painters fall off ladders, postmen are bitten by dogs and eBay sellers get negative feedback; it's an occupational hazard.

As a seller you are quite likely to receive negative feedback. You may choose to respond to the feedback. If so, rather than being aggressive in your response, make a point to all those who may read the comment at a later date; reassure anybody reading it that the negative was a one off, just a mistake and not something to worry about. If you are rude in your response, it may make the situation worse. With this in mind do not follow the example of my feedback responses as I am a little more cynical than I was. With a feedback score in excess of 53,000 the odd neutral or negative won't have too much impact and I can't help being a little cutting in my replies. HOWEVER, this is generally NOT a good idea – grovel and move on.

No matter how many positive feedbacks you earn, customers will always seek out the negative ones, just out of curiosity.

After a year the negative feedback will be removed from your account. If you obtain 2,000 positive feedbacks then a single negative will be ignored so you may see a seller with a 100% record even though they have a negative to their name.

 I received only five negative feedbacks in my first 25,000 ratings. It hurt the first time, but as a seller you get used to it and a small number of negatives should not impact your trading activity.

Extending your customer relationship

Once you have traded successfully with your buyer, you will have started a relationship with them and it is possible to nurture this and hopefully turn them into a loyal customer. It is important not to send any unsolicited emails as this is treated as spam. There are, however, a few things that you may like to try:

- Permission-based campaigns. On your dispatch email, consider a line which says something like, "If you would like details of all our forthcoming sales, please let us know and we will send you a regular update." If the buyer responds, you have their permission to send them emails in the future. What you include in these emails is up to you, but you should find that it will stimulate interest in your eBay activities and any other online sales you may have.

- Newsletter. You may consider a customer newsletter. This could contain hints and tips on eBay, links to help sites, anything really. It could also contain 'Affiliate sales links', which I will discuss in the next few pages. eBay shop owners can send emails to customers who subscribe; these are an ideal way to create awareness of sales and promotions.

- Start your own eBay bulletin. It's a great way to promote yourself and your business.

Affiliate sales

The area of affiliate sales is huge and can produce significant revenue. Many companies such as Amazon, for example, will pay owners of websites a commission for business that is passed to them via live links. Almost anybody with a website or blog can apply to become an affiliate, usually through a third party who will administer the account and payments. CJ Affiliate (www.cj.com) manages the affiliate schemes for many household names and may have one that would be of interest to you.

eBay have their own in-house affiliate scheme and will also pay a commission for any business passed to them from an external website. Check out the eBay Partner Network (www.eBaypartnernetwork.com) and see if it would be of interest to you.

How it works

Affiliate schemes are usually managed by an intermediate company who provides all of the activity tracking for the advertiser and provides all the banners and text links that will be required by the web master. As an affiliate you will have access to these banners and text links and will be able to place them on your website.

When a visitor to your website clicks on a banner or link, a cookie will be stored on their computer. This cookie is not harmful to your visitor; it just contains your affiliate information.

The eBay programs pay their affiliates using the Quality Click Pricing (QCP) payout system. Affiliates will be paid for each click that is directed to an eBay site and the price paid per click will be dependent on the quality of the traffic delivered to eBay. This does sound quite complicated and it is; the primary aim is to send as much traffic as possible to eBay. Quite how they work out commission is a mystery to me.

If such a transaction takes place, the cookie will capture this information and update your affiliate records, crediting you with the reward for the particular action.

It is also possible to display live listings on your own website – as a 'virtual eBay'. This will promote your listings and at the same time may generate extra revenuc for you.

You can build an entire website purely to make money in this way and there are some commercially available packages to help you do it. Virtual eBay stores can be created with a software package such as Build a Niche Store (www.buildanichestore.com). For around £50 you can buy the software, build the stores and stock them with current eBay items. For every purchase made as a result of a visit to your store, you will be paid a commission.

Where it can be used

Affiliate links can be used from almost any website. As you surf around the internet, you will notice links to other sites; it is quite likely that the site owner will receive a payment for passing traffic. All of the big websites use this method to raise funds and can even be rewarded on the number of page impressions that they achieve.

These links can also be used within your email signature. You could have a line that reads 'Please check out my eBay site'. This would include an HTML link as used in the previous section and incorporate your affiliate user ID. If the recipient of the email does click and then transact on eBay, you may well have generated revenue by just replying to an email.

PowerSeller status

As your volume of sales increases, or if the value of those sales reaches a certain level and is maintained for a period of time, you may be invited to become a PowerSeller.

The PowerSeller programme has lost some of its sparkle recently as eBay have removed the badge of office from sellers' listings and downgraded discount levels. However, I still feel it is worth going for.

Membership to the PowerSeller programme is free and there are five levels to aspire to: Bronze, Silver, Gold, Platinum and Titanium. Each level requires a seller to meet and maintain either a pre-set level of average gross sales or a pre-set quantity of items sold, thankfully not both, for the past three months of selling activity.

If you're not a PowerSeller yet, you can always work your way up by meeting these requirements:

- Be registered with eBay for at least 90 days.
- Be registered as a business seller on eBay.co.uk or eBay.ie.
- Have an account in good financial standing.
- Maintain a positive Feedback of 98% or higher over the past 12 months.
- Follow all eBay policies.

- Have a minimum of sales volume of £1,000 per 12 months (based on sales to UK and IE buyers).

- Receive at least a 4.60 average from UK and IE buyers across all four detailed seller ratings (DSRs).

- For all transactions with UK and IE buyers, have no more than 1% of transactions with low DSRs (1s or 2s) on item as described, and a maximum of 2% of low DSRs on communication, dispatch time, and P&P cost.

- For all transactions with UK and IE buyers, have no more than 1.00% of transactions result in opened eBay cases and PayPal Buyer Protection cases, and no more than 0.3% of transactions result in closed cases without seller resolution.

Note: Only transactions to buyers in the UK and Ireland count towards the minimum sales requirement.

Wow, complicated or what? To be honest it is not worth spending too much time on these criteria, if you meet all of the above then you will be informed by eBay. Under new rules introduced in August 2014 it is no longer a requirement to be a PowerSeller in order to benefit from seller discounts.

Membership to the PowerSeller programme does allow access to the PowerSeller discussion boards which can be very helpful. There is the possibility that eBay may phase out the PowerSeller programme as Top-rated seller is now the method by which sellers are judged. If this does happen, I will report the details via my eBay bulletin – be sure to sign up for your copy.

I am currently a Gold PowerSeller for my cosmetics, Silver for my DIY and toys and a Bronze PowerSeller for the 'odds and sods' selling ID.

Do not underestimate the importance of volume sales; higher volumes can keep you in the game even if the monetary value falls.

 I have now been a PowerSeller for about eight years and a Top-rated seller almost non-stop since the scheme began. I believe that it does provide my customers with the confidence that I will deliver on my promises and treat every trade, regardless of value, as they would expect. I am very proud of it – there is a lot of hard work involved to keep at this high level.

Trading worldwide

As your UK business continues to grow, you may well consider exporting your products to the wider European Union and worldwide. Each of these new markets will offer increased business opportunities, but will also require more research to manage the trade restrictions and legislation that may apply. As an example, it is no longer possible to send perfumes, nail varnish and a host of other items outside of the UK. It has something to do with transportation by air and safety. The why is not really important, knowing that this is the case will affect your buying activity and for me it means no more perfume sets at Christmas.

Whilst I will not enter into great depth on this subject, there are a few main areas that need to be addressed. The good news is that there are established bodies that will assist with commercial ventures outside of the UK.

Exporting to the EU

Selling your goods into Europe has fewer restrictions than exporting worldwide and there is no need for any specific customs documentation.

The EU has rapidly expanded, with Cyprus, the Czech Republic, Estonia, Hungary, Latvia, Lithuania, Malta, Poland, the Slovak Republic and Slovenia joining in 2004. Romania and Bulgaria then joined in 2007. This should now make trading with these countries a little easier. The Royal Mail treats a number of other countries as being within Europe so postage charges may not be as high as you would expect.

Some specific goods may require additional documentation and your chosen carrier may also have some paperwork to complete.

It is worth noting that when you send packages to dependencies of EU member states, such as the Falkland Islands, full customs documentation will be required.

When trading internationally, it is important to keep in mind exchange rate considerations. If the euro is performing well against the pound, for example, UK goods will be cheaper in the euro zone, which is an opportunity to increase your sales to the continent. The value of the US dollar against the British pound is another important figure that it is worth keeping an eye on.

Exporting worldwide

Opening up the world as your marketplace does entail more paperwork. When using the standard Royal Mail services, a simple customs label can be attached to the parcel; this contains a description of the item, the value and the weight, and will be signed by you. If using another carrier for your items, there may be additional information required. Add a note to your eBay listings to inform international buyers that they may be liable to import duties based on the value of their purchase.

The list below is just an example of some of the things that may be needed.

- Import licence. As certain goods require an import licence, check with your importer that they have all the necessary documentation before you export your goods to them.

- Export licence. Certain goods going to some countries will require an export licence. Visit gov.uk for more information.

- Certificates of origin. Certificates of origin and movement certificates should be available from larger chambers of commerce. If the country you are trading with has a preferential trade agreement, you may receive reduced tariff rates or even duty free treatment.

- VAT labels/clearance. If you are exporting outside of the EU, each item over £100 must carry a VAT Label 444 on the outside of the package. These are available from your local Customs VAT office.

- Commercial invoice. If you are sending goods other than samples, gifts or possessions to destinations outside of the EU, three copies of a commercial invoice must accompany each package.

Who can help?

For any advice relating to the shipment of goods overseas, contact HMRC (hmrc.gov.uk).

Summary

You should now:

- Understand eBay's shops and seller tools.

- Understand why your feedback is so important.

- Understand what affiliate sales are.

- Know how to become a PowerSeller.

- Understand some of the paperwork required to export to the EU and worldwide.

If you are like me, you should find that the fun bit of eBay is the buying and the selling. But the supporting paperwork can't be ignored. So, if you can contain your excitement, legal issues and tax are coming right up in Chapter 10.

TEN

MANAGING THE PAPERWORK

Overview

Not surprisingly, you will find that there is a certain amount of administration required to run your own business. If nothing else, you will need to know how much profit you are making so that you can alter your selling strategy accordingly. There is also the question of tax that may be due on any profits made through your eBay transactions.

As a seller on eBay, you have agreed to comply with all applicable domestic and international laws and regulations regarding your use of the eBay service; this is a condition of registration and applies to all of your listings.

You are also responsible for paying all fees associated with using the eBay site. This means that if you are trading as a business then it is your responsibility to pay any taxes on your earnings. eBay will not manage this for you and if asked by HMRC they will make any relevant information about your trading available.

This section outlines the basics of managing your paperwork and covers the areas of taxation and self-employment. This is a complex area and tax situations are different for each individual, so it is important to seek professional guidance regarding your own circumstances.

Business plan

When you set out to trade on eBay, you may have a firm idea of where you want to go and have the necessary funding in place to achieve it. There may, however, come a time when you will need to convince other people that your business is a good prospect – for example, if you need to borrow money from a bank.

When this time comes, you will be expected to have a business plan of some description. Below I outline the basics of such a document.

What is a business plan?

Put simply, a business plan is a written document that sets out the future intentions of a business and shows how it is to evolve and grow. A business plan will outline the goals for the future, what resources will be needed to achieve them and how the resources will be utilised. These resources could include people as well as accommodation and equipment. Above all, the business plan will tell the reader why the business will succeed. The desired outcome is that if ever you need to acquire funding the reader is so impressed that they part with the cash.

What sort of things go into a business plan?

There is no fixed format for a business plan. The main thing is for it to contain the right elements presented in a concise way. Some of the elements that should be included are:

- Executive summary. This will summarise the whole document into one or two pages and is intended for those readers who have little time to read through the whole document; if they like the executive summary, they will read any extra detail they need. Although it appears first, it is a summary and should be written last.

- Introduction. An introduction or overview of the business or business idea. This should provide the reader with an insight on where the business is now.

- Competition. This will provide the reader with an overview of the marketplace in which the business operates and any competition that it must face.

- Services offered. In the case of an eBay business, this section is likely to contain details of products that are currently, or could be, sold via eBay as a route to market.

- Strategy section. Outline the way in which the business will market its products and how it will price them and distribute them to the end customer. Maybe you will choose to advertise your eBay business in the traditional press or on the radio.

- Financial plan. This section will include balance sheets, cash flow statements and predictions for income and expenditure.

  To expand on that final element, the financial plan includes:
- Balance sheet. A balance sheet makes the comparison between what your business owns (its assets), against what it owes (its debts).

- Cash flow statement. A cash flow statement shows how you intend to cope during periods when you will be buying stock and may not be selling it at the same rate. Preparing for the Christmas rush would be an example: you will buy lots of stock in the months before, but not receive any income from sales until some time later. The cash flow statement will show how you will manage this situation.

- Income statement. An income statement will compare your income (sales from eBay), against expenditure (both stock purchase and business costs). This will demonstrate if you are actually going to make any money from the undertaking.

Having a business plan in place is a good idea even if you are not looking for additional finance. It will force you to focus on the hard facts of your business and allow you to take steps to correct things if they start to go wrong. If you don't have a plan for your business, how will you know if you are successful?

Legal concerns

The legal issues surrounding trading in any form can be quite complex; this section is intended only as a guide. You should consult a qualified professional if you are in any doubt as to the legality of your venture.

Buyers at online auctions have less protection under consumer law than through traditional retail outlets or fixed-price eBay listings – the phrase caveat emptor (buyer beware) holds true. However, there are some areas, such as the deliberate failure to send an item that has been purchased at auction, which are criminal offences. Citizens Advice can offer help with issues like this (www.citizensadvice.org.uk).

Governing law and legal compliance

The eBay User Agreement states the conditions under which you have agreed to trade and details eBay's position in areas such as the law and taxation. The full agreement can be found in the eBay help pages; I have copied below some of the main points.

Extracts from the eBay User Agreement

- This User Agreement shall be governed by and construed in accordance with English law and subject to the exclusive jurisdiction of the English courts.
- Please note, that your country (and/or that of any user you deal with) may have laws which apply to your transactions with other users regardless of what you agree with us (now) or with that user (later).
- The laws of your country may be different from English law, including laws governing what can be legally offered, sold, exported, bought or imported.
- There may be additional legal requirements, relating to (for example) the requirement to hold a licence to buy or sell certain items, or to register a transfer in a central registry. You shall comply with all applicable domestic

and international laws, statutes, ordinances and regulations regarding your use of our service and your bidding on, listing, purchase and solicitation of offers to purchase and sale of items.

- There is no practical way for us (eBay) to continually monitor the laws of every country, or each user transaction. Please do not assume that you are allowed to do what other users do, or that we are approving or validating any transaction, even if you have successfully made similar sales or purchases in the past.

These few lines are really saying that it is down to the individual to ensure that they comply with all rules and legal requirements when trading. eBay will make certain help sections available and offer general advice, but cannot advise on an individual situation.

Insurance

Trusting in your existing home insurance to provide the cover for your eBay business can lead to unnecessary stress and inconvenience at the time of a claim. It is not necessarily the insurer's concerns over the level of stock but more the type of stock and liability claims that may arise from this (referred to as product liability). Some professions may result in more insurance claims, for example, carrying large amounts of stock may encourage unwelcome attention from thieves, or allowing collection from your premises might result in an increased risk of public liability claims.

Direct insurers only sell their own products and, as with comparison websites, it can prove difficult to get the exact cover you need or to be made aware of additional options. I am a firm believer that insurance should be sought from an independent insurance broker who takes the time to understand the cover needed. An average figure for cover is around £250 pa.

Employing the kids

Over the past few years a number of experts have offered their services free of charge to readers of my weekly eBay Bulletin.

As I am very mean I wanted to know just how little I could pay my kids and still avoid jail. Here is the official word:

> "Some 60% of UK businesses are family owned and many of us are aware of the possibility of employing a spouse or partner in our family business in order to reduce our year end tax bill with some extra wage costs.

That's all very well, but what about the kids? Can we pay them a salary too? Our children have a tax/NI free personal allowance, so can we use this to our advantage?

The simple answer is 'Yes', so here are a few of the basics:

The Children And Young Person's Act states that no person under 13 years of age may be employed, other than in very specific areas, such as acting, modelling and sporting activities; so employing your 8-year-old as head of marketing could raise a few questions.

Under current legislation, the National Minimum Wage doesn't need to be paid to workers in the family business, provided they are members of the employer's family, and share the family home. That said, the more we can pay them, within reason, the greater the expense for tax purposes.

As with most things, common sense is the watchword here. We need to be able to credibly argue that our kids are performing tasks that are well within their capabilities. Many, these days, are highly computer literate, and may have done work for us on our websites, spread sheets, etc. Others may have helped us with dispatching goods, filling mail shot envelopes, etc.

So, as long as our kids are over 13, and they perform appropriate tasks within our business for a sensible salary, there is nothing to stop us paying them for work done in order to reduce our business tax liability.

There is a wealth of legislation governing this, but, for most of us, it's definitely worth some serious consideration."

I loved this answer and now exploit my kids whenever I can, apart from buying their cars, holidays, clothes, computers and Ugg boots!

Taxation

As more and more trade is passed through eBay, the potential loss to HMRC through unpaid taxes is set to rise. It is therefore quite likely that more attention will be given to traders on eBay by HMRC.

As a general rule, there is no tax liability on any money raised by selling your own items. So, clearing the house or garage of your own possessions should not interest the taxman. He will, however, be interested if you buy with the intention to sell – any profits from this activity are subject to income tax.

The tax rules that apply to an individual could be very complex and this is not the place to delve too deeply into the finer points of tax law. The responsibility lies with the individual to declare their activities to HMRC.

There are three taxes to consider:

1. Income tax.
2. Capital gains tax.
3. VAT.

These are discussed briefly below.

1. Income tax

Income tax is a... tax on income – no surprises there! In the case of an eBay business, this is the profit, after expenses, on any difference between the buying and selling price.

The structure of income tax in the UK operates via a system of bands and allowances. Each individual has a personal allowance which is deducted from their total income in order to arrive at their taxable income. This first chunk of your income is tax free. The rest is then taxable and is subject to different tax rates depending upon the tax band that income falls within. For the latest rates, visit: www.hmrc.gov.uk/rates/it.htm

It is important to note that earnings figures include all income for the year. If you are also employed, then both the income from your job and from eBay will count towards your total earnings.

The actual level at which tax becomes payable, and the rate of that tax payment, will depend upon your personal situation. If you are in any doubt, contact HM Revenue & Customs (www.hmrc.gov.uk) directly and they will advise.

2. Capital gains tax (CGT)

CGT is a tax on the increase in the capital value of an item. You normally only have to pay CGT when you no longer own an asset, that is, when you have disposed of it. This is HMRC's definition and the ruling applies to most assets that are bought and then sold for a higher value: it is the difference between the purchase and sale price that may be liable to tax.

Each individual has a personal allowance, which varies from year to year. There is also an indexation allowance calculator which is used for assets that were purchased some years ago. As a general rule, only high value items will be considered for capital gains. Visit the HMRC website for more information about the circumstances in which capital gains tax might need to be paid (www.hmrc.gov.uk/rates/cgt.htm).

3. VAT

If your taxable turnover, **not just your profit**, hits the VAT threshold, or you expect it to, you must register with HMRC for VAT. VAT is a tax on consumer expenditure and is collected on business transactions.

For a couple of years I deliberately kept the turnover of my cosmetics business under the VAT threshold (which is at £81,000 as of April 2014), which meant I virtually shut down after Christmas until the new tax year. VAT is calculated on a rolling 12-month period so I also had to keep track of my sales on a monthly basis and shut up shop when business was too good.

Finally in March 2012 I decided to take the plunge and register. I knew that I could increase my turnover well beyond the registration limit so although VAT would now be charged on all my turnover it was effectively the doorway to increased sales.

VAT has now become a way of life and I guess we should all be thankful that it is only 20%. It is not so attractive if you are a trader whose turnover is just over the registration threshold. Adding an extra 20% to your selling price – especially on eBay where other sellers may not need to and where price is a very sensitive issue. The bottom line is that if you want to increase your turnover then VAT is the price you have to pay in order to access the next level.

If you are close to the limit and destined to exceed it then try to burst right through and at least get some benefit from paying the extra levy. I took on a third cosmetic brand just prior to registration and my turnover leapt from £77,000 to £160,000 in the first year.

The full-blown VAT scheme can be quite arduous, with the need to record VAT paid on stock and services and VAT charged on sales. The numbers are crunched and payment made based on the outcome. It is, however, possible to adopt a flat rate scheme, whereby input and output VAT are ignored and a straight percentage of your turnover is sent to the HMRC each quarter. With this there is no need to keep or manage any paperwork.

Each market sector has its own flat rate of VAT and for retail cosmetics it is 8%. This suits me fine as I don't always obtain a VAT receipt for purchases made and under the flat rate scheme I don't need a receipt. As a sweetener HMRC offers a 1% discount for the first year but does, however, impose a turnover restriction of £150,000, plus the VAT paid. In subsequent years the 1% is added back on to your rate but the turnover limit rises to £230,000 (figures as of 2014; be sure to check the current values).

There is a little good news as VAT is not paid on eBay fees for those who are registered – it's all to do with a ruling about trades between European companies, confusing but useful. eBay is registered in Luxembourg with a VAT rate of 15%, so your fees will go down. It works like this: eBay charge you, say, 10% as a final value fee (FVF), which includes VAT charged at the Luxemburg rate of 15%. As a UK VAT registered business you don't have to pay this and can instruct eBay to bill you without any VAT added. So a sale of £6.99 will incur a FVF of £0.607431 instead of £0.699 – a saving of just over 9p.

When I registered for VAT the inspector came to call just to make sure all was in order and that I was intending to continue trading and not just pulling a VAT scam. An interesting point is that you claim any VAT paid on stock in hand at the time of registration. I did try to shorten the visit by holding the meeting in the conservatory at HQ. I knew that when the sun came around it would heat up quickly so I wore shorts and plied the inspector with hot drinks. Sure enough the business was soon concluded. Remember Arkwright and the mouse?

One final point about the dreaded VAT is that because your turnover will decrease by an amount, in my case 8%, then your net profits before tax will also decrease, thus reducing your income tax or corporation tax liability. There you go – VAT is not quite the huge, mean beast you first thought.

Most business transactions involve the supply of goods or services. VAT is payable if they are:

• Supplies made in the United Kingdom or the Isle of Man.

• By a taxable person.

• In the course of a business.

• Not specifically exempted or zero-rated.

If your business turnover has exceeded the VAT threshold, or you expect it might, contact the HMRC helpline on 0845 010 9000.

eBay offer some advice on this area; however, the burden of responsibility rests with the individual. I have extracted some of their key points regarding VAT and pasted them below:

• Laws and regulations dealing with VAT on sales transactions are complicated. These laws and regulations address, for example, whether a seller's business should be registered for VAT, whether a seller is required to charge VAT on sold items, and, if so, how much VAT should be charged on those items.

• For the above reason, a seller should consult an independent tax advisor and/or local tax authority to determine what laws and rules apply, including whether a business should be registered and whether and how much VAT is required to be charged on an item.

- For UK sellers, as a first research step, a seller may find it useful to consult the HMRC web site, which addresses certain aspects of VAT and VAT registration.

- As an online marketplace, eBay leaves the decision to the seller as to whether and how VAT should be charged on an item. eBay, however, does require the seller to adhere to all applicable VAT laws and regulations in listing an item on www.eBay.co.uk.

- In the item description, the seller should set out clearly the amount or percentage of VAT that will be charged.

- If there is no mention of VAT in the item description, the seller should not add VAT to the final item price. In such a case, if VAT is legally due, the seller bears the responsibility of paying that VAT to the appropriate authorities according to any applicable laws and regulations. Again, if there is any question as to the seller's VAT responsibilities, the seller should consult an independent tax advisor and/or local tax authority.

- You will need to submit a quarterly return to the VAT guys and then settle within five weeks of the end of the quarter. Payment has to be by electronic methods but to be honest the whole process is dead easy. Painful, but straightforward.

- I employ a bookkeeper to submit VAT returns on my behalf. Although I could easily do this myself, the cost is just £15 per quarter (tax deductible) and I like the idea of having somebody to chase me for the figures and act as an intermediary.

Self-employment

Once your activities on eBay have reached a certain level, it may be the time to register as self-employed. This will probably occur when you have sold all of your own personal items and decide to begin trading: buying with the intention to sell for a profit.

This can seem daunting and there may be a temptation to continue as before. However, the process is not too difficult and there are some benefits as well. In this section I will expand on the topic of becoming self-employed. As mentioned before, I cannot be specific about personal tax situations as they will vary from person to person. If you need to confirm your own circumstances, check the HMRC website (www.hmrc.gov.uk/startingup).

If you are newly self-employed you can phone this number: 0845 915 4515. Give them your details over the phone – such as your address, National

Insurance number, business name, etc., – and they will pass your details on to the tax office for you. No form filling!

If eBay is your main source of income then you may be entitled to working tax credit. Contact your local tax office for more details.

What does it mean?

Becoming self-employed on eBay simply means that you intend to buy and sell for profit. As with any earned income, you will need to declare this to HMRC. It also means that any costs involved with your eBay activities can be offset against your profit, as it is the figure after the deduction of expenses that may be liable to income tax.

Self-employment is just the method to capture all the details of your eBay activities and record them in a simple way.

You can be self-employed and also work full-time or part-time elsewhere. All of your net income is added together and income tax is applied depending upon your personal circumstances. If eBay is to be your only source of income then you can earn up to your personal tax free allowance before paying any tax. Watch out for National Insurance though, as this kicks in at a lower level.

Where to go for more help

Working from home does have its advantages – a six-yard commute to the shed beats the M25 any day – but it can also throw up questions about tax, regulations and so on. Visit Enterprise Nation (www.enterprisenation.com) for up-to-date help and advice about home working written by home workers.

The Enterprise Nation website is free (which is always a good start) and packed full of news and information about working from home.

How do I register?

The first thing to do is register with HMRC. There is, naturally, a booklet about it – 'Thinking of Working for Yourself'. This contains some basic information to read before you register, which you should do within three months of the date you began working for yourself. You can register online at: www.hmrc.gov.uk.

HMRC will then send a starter pack with more details. This form will also cover the issues surrounding National Insurance contributions.

National Insurance

National Insurance contributions build up your entitlements to various benefits, such as unemployment benefit and the state retirement pension.

There are several different types of National Insurance contributions that you might have to pay. For the self-employed, there are four main types and these are all explained on the HMRC website: www.hmrc.gov.uk/rates/nic.htm

It is also worth noting that if your expected earnings for the year fall below a certain amount you may be eligible for an exemption from Class 2 payments. To apply for this exemption, just contact HMRC and – you've guessed it – there is a form to fill in.

How to record your business activities

You will need to submit details of your trading activities to HMRC. This is most likely to occur at the end of the tax year in April, although you will have several months to actually fill the form in. If you have kept some simple records during the year you will only have to copy a few figures into your tax return. HMRC are unlikely to want to see your detailed records.

How you record your business activities is really down to personal choice. There are some computer packages available or you could consult an accountant or bookkeeper. You could also create your own spreadsheet or just write them down on paper. You must decide how best to do this, but once you have settled on a method keep your records up to date – this will make filling in your tax return much easier.

If you don't have any business management software you can of course use eBay to help you keep track of your sales. In your My eBay you probably already use the 'Sold' section to see how your items are selling; these details can be printed out to provide a permanent record of trading activity. You can customise the content of the reports contained within the 'File management centre' and use this to compile your trading figures for the year.

Access to the file management centre is via a link in the seller tools section of My eBay. Here you can ask eBay to send you a download of your active listings and sales records – just select the type of report you want and wait for it to arrive in your inbox. Take things one step further and schedule downloads on a regular basis, store them away and form filling will be a whole lot easier.

PayPal also has some very handy records in its History section. If this is your only payment method then the PayPal records could be all you need as a sales figure. Using the PayPal receipts sorts out the issue of refunds and also non-payers so it makes life a little easier.

Following my decision to turn the Mollybol cosmetic business into a limited company in June 2013 I started using a finance package – Kashflow. This online system can be accessed by my accountant and used to compile accounts for Companies House. It costs £12 per month and is simple enough to use after the usual blundering around period.

At this time I do not use management software to compile my accounts for the toy and DIY business; my turnover is such that a simple spreadsheet is sufficient.

I have found that printing the sales on a monthly basis works well for me. I can then put the kettle on and update my spreadsheet during a quiet time, including my trading costs and expenses. This will in turn provide my trading figures for my tax return.

If you would like a copy of the spreadsheet I use, send an email to Mollybol@eBaybulletin.co.uk and I'll forward it on to you.

The system is a little labour intensive, but it works for me. Sometimes simple is best.

How to work out your business profit

There are three main elements that will determine how your business performs. These form your trading account and will determine if you have made a profit or a loss.

1. You will make sales via eBay and the value of these when added together will produce your turnover. Turnover also includes any postage you charge, insurance and so on; it is the total of monies you receive.

2. The items you sell will cost you something to purchase; the total value of these purchases will be your cost of sales. When you deduct the cost of your sales from the turnover you will have calculated your gross profit.

3. Just buying and selling is only part of the picture. It will cost you something to sell your goods and it will have cost you something to buy them in the first place (e.g. the cost of your internet connection, eBay fees, etc.); these are your expenses. When the expenses are deducted from the gross profit,

you will end up with a net profit figure. This is the true profit that you have made and it is this figure upon which you may have to pay tax and National Insurance.

Typical expenses of an eBay business

In any business the true cost of selling will vary. There are the costs of the stock and the costs of actually selling items and running the business. With an eBay business, the costs can be quite varied, although there are some that would apply to almost all businesses.

These expenses of your business will reduce the amount of profit you make from your trading activities, so it is important to record them all. It is also important not to inflate them as this may cause problems when you submit your tax return.

Typical expenses will include:
• Packing materials.
• Stamps.
• Staff wages.
• Heat and light.
• Insurance.
• Fuel.
• Stationery (paper, ink).
• Telephone lines.
• Bank charges.
• eBay charges.
• PayPal charges.
• Rent.
• Training.

In addition to these running costs, your business will also need some equipment before it can trade. The list of items will vary, but is likely to include:
• Computers.
• Digital cameras.
• Printers.
• Mobile phone.

You may also have buildings that are used for your business, maybe for storage; these will need to be rented or purchased and maintained as well.

Becoming a limited company

June 2013 saw another major landmark for the Mollybol operation as the cosmetics business was incorporated and now trades as a limited company.

This is a whole different ball game and one that I am still getting to grips with, as I learn more I will pass on my findings via my newsletter.

The gist of the new arrangement is that I am now an employee again and also a director of the new company. I now have to submit an expense claim each month for items such as mileage, home working expenses, car parking and so on.

There is also a need to set up a payroll system and a company pension scheme so there's quite a lot to think about. To this end I would strongly recommend taking the services of an accountant if you are going down this road yourself. These guys will set up the company correctly and act as a correspondence address for the first year or so while things settle down. They will compile the company accounts from your shoebox of receipts, but be prepared to pay for this service – I expect to pay around £1,400 per year for the basic service. My accountant also runs the payroll system at a cost of £35 per month.

A business bank account is a must and for this I opted for Barclays and I am most impressed – easy to use, secure and they don't keep trying to sell me stuff.

It is still early days but so far I have found the whole limited company thing very easy to manage and in time it should save me money on income tax and National Insurance.

Summary

You should now:
- Understand the broad terms of trading under eBay's User Agreement.
- Have a broad understanding of the implications of income tax, CGT and VAT on your business.
- Know how to register as self-employed.
- Know the typical expenses of an eBay business.

Conclusion

Welcome to the conclusion of the book and well done for making it this far!

I hope that these pages have been of interest and will increase your eBay profits significantly. A career in any business takes time to develop and eBay is no different. Throughout my eBay journey there have been high points and many lessons to learn, most of which are contained in this book so that you don't fall foul of them.

I also intend to develop further my own eBay business over the coming months and years. This includes overhauling my eBay shops, redesigning my workshop preparation and storage processes and completely re-inventing my photography skills; so this is only really the end of the beginning.

The cosmetics, toys and DIY businesses are up and running but I still have a few ideas. If I sleep less over the coming months I might even get round to developing them.

The great thing about an eBay business is that you can take it at your own pace. If you found a stage in the book that suits you, stop there for a while and see how things go.

The chapter on the listing process is quite detailed and some practice will be needed to present items correctly. But stick with it, the difference it will make to your sales cannot be overstated. The chapters concerning the supply of stock, pre and post-sales processes, coupled with the numerous sales tips along the way, should ensure that you have an edge on your competition.

Please try some of the HTML codes – it is a little like learning a new language. There is still loads that can be achieved by designing your own layout and it should save you a few pounds along the way.

Where should you go for more help?

There are always things to learn and there will always be somebody willing to assist. If you do need more advice, access the eBay community discussion boards or use the navigation techniques you will have picked up from this book to find your way through the maze of eBay help pages.

Why not subscribe to my free weekly newsletter at intel.harriman-house.com/ebay-bulletin? It contains the latest gossip from eBay and loads of hints and tips from my own trading experiences and those of my readers.

eBay is bound to grow, at least for the foreseeable future. What a fantastic time to begin your own business – with almost no capital outlay required, a work pattern that suits your own lifestyle and rewards that are limited only by your own actions.

Welcome to The Good Life

I have fully embraced the lifestyle: the late nights before Christmas packing parcels and the extra coffee breaks during the day. I travelled from a standing start to leaving full-time work within two years – and anybody can do this. As I have said, selling on eBay is not difficult. It is the contents of this book that will place you ahead of the crowd as we rush headlong into a brave new world where every household has an eBay account and the first place you look to buy anything is eBay.

I would like to wish you every success in your future trading and that it brings to you, as it has to me, a glimpse of The Good Life.

Index